EXPAT SECRETS

Success Principles for Business, Manufacturing, and Life

BOB ROBERTSON

Thoughts Alive Publishing
First edition

Expat Secrets

Copyright © 2022 by Bob Robertson. All rights reserved.

No part of this publication may be reproduced, stored in a retrieval system or transmitted in any way by any means, electronic, mechanical, photocopy, recording or otherwise without the prior permission of the author except as provided by USA copyright law.

Thoughts Alive Publishing
www.ThoughtsAlive.com

Printed in the U.S.A.

ISBN 978-0-9816749-9-5 (Hardcover)
ISBN 979-8-9873530-0-4 (Ebook)
ISBN 979-8-9873530-1-1 (Paperback)

CONTENTS

Preface 5

Introduction 7

Chapter 1: Wisconsin, California, Utah 13
    1.0 — The Power of Instrumentation 13
    1.1 — Variation 18
    1.2 — The Flow 25
    1.3 — Honeywell – MOL –
    from Milwaukee to California - Mind Model 29
    1.4 — Determination 38
    1.5 — The Wisdom of Deming 41

Chapter 2: Singapore 51
    2.0 — Willingness to Pivot .51

Chapter 3: Indonesia 61
    3.0 — Plot Twist 61
    3.1 — Perspective 63
    3.2 — Freedoms 66
    3.3 — The Affect 72

Chapter 4: Arizona, New York, Ohio 95
    4.0 — Standing for Quality 95
    4.1 — Why Quality? 98
    4.2 — Statistics, Why? – A Profound Secret! 106
    4.3 — The Joseph Juran Secret(s) 114
    4.4 — Living Behind the Quality Dikes 118
    4.5 — Intuition 121

Chapter 5: Russia 137
    5.0 — Creation of Synchron 137
    5.1 — Russia – Training Education 147
    5.2 — Moscow Train Incident 152
    5.3 — Statistical Quality Control 154
    5.4 — Departure from Kineshma –
    The Painting Episode 156

Chapter 6: Illinois, Nevada, Idaho 195
    6.0 — The Retrofit 195
    6.1 — Personalities 198
    6.2 — Hunt for the Red X – The Shainin System . . . 203
    6.3 — Pre-suasion 205
    6.4 — Constructive Confrontation 207

Conclusion 211

Bonus Fun-Ditties 213

About the Author 217

PREFACE

Welcome to Expat Secrets. I'm Bob Robertson, and in this work, I share memorable experiences and lessons I learned working as a foreigner in various countries. I worked with locals in these efforts, improving quality control systems in their respective industries. As I faced challenges in both my career and personal life, I discovered that the success principles, or secrets, can be applied in both.

The term "Profundity" expresses this work's deep and essential meaning. The beauty of the ideas to follow is marked by simple expressions I've called "Profound Ditties," or shorter still, "Fun-Ditties." Remaining brief, these Fun-Ditties will help the profundity of the work not be lost in the maze of words and ideas we'll explore.

The word expat is short for "expatriate," one who leaves home to live and work in a foreign country funded by a firm or government. It is understood that "home" is somewhere else, and they will likely return.

It is a monumental task to find success as an expat, with differences in technology, language, culture, family, business norms, diet, health issues, etc. Following is my experience as an expat and the success secrets I discovered for both industry and life.

INTRODUCTION

A ROAR went up from the main floor, heard clearly upstairs in the 4,000-worker factory. It was 6:30 am, a half-hour after shift change. What prompted the outburst? Management had just posted production numbers for the third-shift Mold Room!

I was an Expat Engineering Manager at Fairchild in Jakarta, Indonesia. We assembled Plastic Dual-in-line Integrated Circuits (PDIP computer chips). The assembly process included two main steps: the wire bond and then the mold.

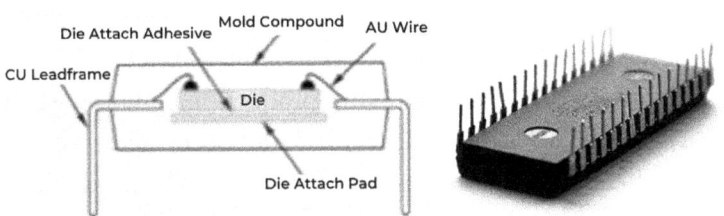

Integrated Circuits Wire Bond / Mold

The first step was upstairs in the two-floor factory, where clean-room conditions were rigorously enforced with face masks and a super-clean environment. The molding operation, which packaged the integrated circuits downstairs, required less scrutiny (no face masks, less air-quality control, and a more relaxed setting).

As we (five new expat managers) began our task, the mold room was a cavalier operation, where twenty minutes before shift change, mold room operators lined up at the time clock. They punched out precisely at the shift end. They somehow timed their activities to coincide with hoorahs and back-slapping at the time clock, jockeying to be first in line.

We stepped in to make a difference. Much of the re-orienting, training, and re-training went on during the weeks and months following. A mindset of how much more could be accomplished before the final buzzer became routine. One significant change included posting in glaring numbers on a wall-sized screen how many units were completed during the shift.

The third shift was routinely the least productive, least directed, and least happy at shift end. But after two and a half years with new expectations, production numbers became profoundly different. Even the third shift caught the vision of production success and how good increased production could make them feel!

So, about that roar. Third-shift production numbers, when posted, were *higher* than they had ever been! They landed higher than even 1st and 2nd shift numbers! The entire first-floor production force witnessed this milestone event, both third-shift leaving and first-shift arriving. The outburst of happiness was felt and expressed by every man and woman in the room.

Total factory production was based on a figure of merit: Leads Per Operator Hour. Since the many integrated circuit

(IC) packages had different numbers of leads, this provided a valid measure of total production output: complete factory performance from both floors. As you can see in the table below, the difference between production per headcount from 1982 to 1984 was significant. Greater production with fewer man hours was the goal, and it had been accomplished gloriously.

	1982	1984
LPOH (Leads per Operator Hour)	890	5,201
Production Headcount	4,056	2,425

This difference (higher production with reduced headcount) elicited the throaty roar from downstairs when the company posted the production numbers. The change was favorable for corporate management, also bringing an outcry from the board room! Contrast the days of operators lining up at the time clock, with now, where they instead are lining up to see the shift-end production numbers. It was magical.

What secret sauce was employed to get this positive change? Is it something anyone can use, or is it limited to a select few? To answer this, let's first examine what the term Secret means and how it relates to our story. Here are a few possibilities:

"Secret" definition:

a) Hidden – known only to a few
b) Mystery – unexplained
c) Covert – done, so no one notices
d) Underhanded – fraudulently or with deception

e) Furtive – slyly or with stealth
f) Surreptitious – action skillfully done secretly

As the name of this book is "Expat Secrets," let's explore which of the above definitions relates to our use of the term.

a) Was our strategy Hidden?
No, the production crew voicing their approval rules out the Hidden option. Our success (and method of arriving there) was not kept from the team, as everyone was involved, playing their part.

b) Was the strategy a Mystery?
Not even remotely, with management working for months for this change to take root. Instead, it was intentional and calculated.

c) Was the strategy Covert?
Certainly not. Everyone noticed the changes and the outcomes, as evidenced by the shouting to the world about their favorable results.

d-f) Was the strategy Underhanded? Furtive? Surreptitious?
That the endeavor took place above board eliminates deception. It was not accomplished slyly nor secretly. There was no stealth or fraud.

So, why do I use the term "Secret" to describe our production success? The answer to this question lies in the pages to come. Our team followed dependable principles to achieve remarkable outcomes on the assembly line. Soon, I will explain how the same principles can be applied to life for similarly impressive results.

Fun-Ditty #0.1

> *"It's not the will to win, but the will to prepare to win that makes the difference."*
> *- Paul 'Bear' Bryant (1913-1983)*
> *American College Football Coach*

CHAPTER 1

Wisconsin, California, Utah

1.0 — The Power of Instrumentation

I grew up in a town with a population of 1,000, where the nearest large town was over 120 miles away. As a fifth grader in the late 1940s, I sold small bags of popcorn outside the town's one movie theater long before refreshments were served inside, which, for me, seemed to be a good way to make a buck. Some smart-aleck seventh grader asked one night if I was making any money, and I proudly pulled a handful of change out of my pocket, to which he asked, how much of that is profit? I went home that night and asked Dad, "…what is profit?"

In the coffee shop next to my dad's two-pump service station was a small card taped to the cash register which read:

A friend is not a fellow who is taken in by sham,
A friend is one who knows your
faults and doesn't give a damn.

In that small town, we knew everyone, faults and all, and it made a lot of sense. Steve may have been stepping out on his wife, but we could depend on him if we ever needed help. We had plenty of friends. However, Dad told me I'd be happy to count my true friends on one hand.

My perspective of that "friend" quote did change when I had my children. I gave more than a damn how they turned out.

I served two years in the US Army at White Sands Missile Range in New Mexico on the Redstone Missile program. We were engaged in the high-tension space race, leading to Russian cosmonaut Yuri Gagarin's first man-in-space event in April 1961, completing one full orbit of the earth.

Yuri Gagarin – Russia's first man-in-space and the 43-meter titanium monument erected in his honor in Moscow.

The space race had only heightened the world's consciousness towards success, achievement, excellence, and pushing our limits. There was an urgency to thrive not just in the space industry but in every sector. There was a hyper-focus on proving to the world that your enterprise wasn't just meeting needs; it needed to exceed expectations. At the same time, individuals were feeling the same pressure. Are we, as a society of individuals, measuring up, or are we failing to exceed the expectations we've heaped on ourselves?

It is a timeless concern that only seems to intensify with each new generation. But when we discover the principles that govern success, there is no need to scramble or fight against the world for relevance or impressiveness. We can merely follow time-tested principles, and the success we seek becomes a natural by-product.

Sometimes, however, life-changing principles are only discovered by first experiencing their effects inside the various microcosms of work or service environments and extrapolating how they can be applied in the bigger picture.

Following the Army service, I married my sweetheart, then struggled through the university, earning a Bachelor of Science in Electrical Engineering. My first job out of school was in Milwaukee with AC Spark Plug, a division of General Motors, on the Titan missile program, in the heyday of "Sputnik" fervor. Kennedy had declared war on the lack of scientific minds. It was an exciting time in international politics.

While working at AC, a co-worker and I collaborated on an electronics text and signed an agreement with Prentice-Hall in 1967. I also met a teacher who encouraged me to apply for a night position at his vocational school (now called the Milwaukee Institute of Technology). I did and entered my first teaching experience with stage fright but hung on, coming to love the effort.

Later, when a full-time position opened, I left the missile program industry and spent five years teaching instrumentation, described by Merriam-Webster dictionary as "the installation, maintenance, and calibration of devices used in the automation of industrial processes." It was a strange turn, having just received a commendation from General Motors for work on a Titan missile guidance & control package. But I had found my niche in the classroom.

Instrumentation. It was a work centered around measuring a variable, such as pressure, temperature, flow, force, humidity, etc., comparing the measurement with a desired (target) value, and then making corrections to move the variable closer to the target. As I learned how to explain the powers, problems, and potential brilliance in an industry that instrumentation can achieve to my students, I was unaware of how the concept would serve me much later when I would become an expat in Indonesia. It served me even in my personal life for many years to come.

To explain, let's explore something called Instrumentation Loops, where a physical process is controlled or kept at the desired value.

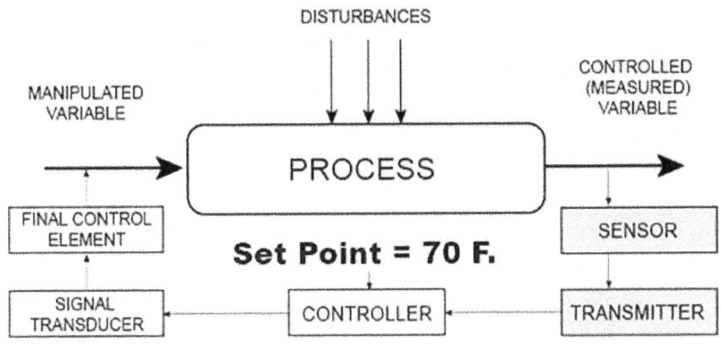

Physical Control Block Diagram

Suppose you want a process temperature to be held at a setpoint of 70 degrees. Consider the diagram shown here. The sensor (controlled variable) is transmitted to the controller, where the actual temperature is then compared to the desired value or setpoint. Any difference between the two sends a corrective signal to manipulate the final control element, bringing the process temp to the setpoint.

This scheme works for *any* process requiring control! If you want to control the temperature in your home at 70 degrees, there will be multiple disturbances, from outside temperature changes to the kids leaving a window open. The control loop in your home takes care of it, with the thermostat turning the furnace on and off at that setpoint.

There are thousands of instrumentation loops in mechanical operations, with dozens in your home and automobiles. But we, as humans, have instrumentation loops built into our design as well. The vision for our life and the goals we aim to achieve are our setpoints. And if we allow it, our internal GPS or compass (otherwise known as our intuition, inspiration, or gut instinct) can be the instrumentation that keeps us heading in the right direction, despite any external disturbances we will encounter.

Fun-Ditty #1.0

> *"If one advances confidently in the direction of his dreams, and endeavors to live the life which he has imagined, he will meet with a success unexpected in common hours."*
>
> *- Henry David Thoreau*

1.1 — Variation

As I continued my work in the automation of industrial processes, I discovered another principle that governs not just success in manufacturing, but also success in life.

All things in life vary. We make decisions daily based on the variation around us. The variation we expect to see in our results is due to *common*, natural causes. Basic human error, nature, and factors outside of our control can all play a part. It's when variation is larger than expected that we look for *special* causes. Special causes are factors for which we do have meaningful control.

One key to success in manufacturing, business, and life is understanding the variation's information and the difference between *common* and *special* causes. Our response to *special* causes must be different from our response to *common* causes. Attempts to reduce the *common* cause always tends to *increase* the problem, while attempts to reduce *special* causes tends to *decrease* the problem.

To illustrate this principle, imagine a funnel fixed at the top of a post, through which marbles are dropped and their landing spot near the X on the ground is marked.

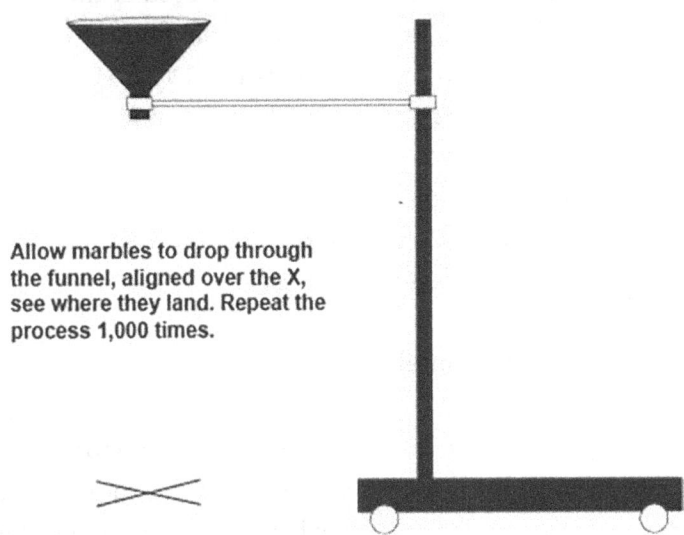

Allow marbles to drop through the funnel, aligned over the X, see where they land. Repeat the process 1,000 times.

From the top view over the X, we map the spot where the marbles landed. The results of this experiment are shown on the left in the next image, and illustrate a natural range of variation from a stable system. The pattern is regular, with no dramatic outliers. This is characteristic of common cause variation.

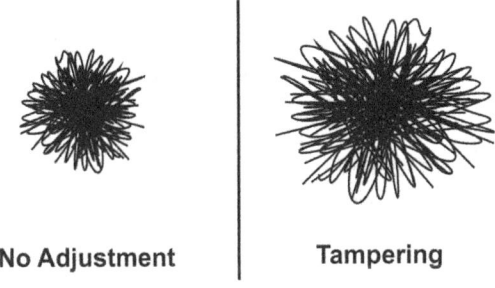

No Adjustment | Tampering

But what if, with an intent to reduce the pattern of variation, we move the funnel based on where the marble landed on the last drop? Will actively compensating for common variations be helpful? In other words, if the drop occurred at the top of the pattern (12 o'clock), what if we move the funnel toward 6 o'clock for the next drop, etc.? The tampering pattern illustrated on the right occurs when, after each drop, the funnel is moved to counter the last drop.

As you can see, tampering with the system results in a much more chaotic, wider range of variation than if we had just let things be. The lesson here is this:

Don't Touch that Funnel!

This principle of letting things BE is important in manufacturing operations, but equally applicable in parenting, marriage, and any other system where results are observable. Common cause variations will always be present, and we conserve energy and preserve predictability by putting our attention to only *special* cause variations.

An example from sports can illustrate this principle. In shooting baskets, sometimes even the best, most practiced players will get the ball in with only net, while sometimes the ball will hit the rim on its way in. A good coach will overlook the rim-hitting throws because the overall results are still acceptable, and intervention there may increase the player's anxiety and worsen the results. Natural variation doesn't always require drastic intervention.

To help us understand this further, we can look at Normal Distribution. If the results of an operation or experiment are measurable, we can observe the results in a bell-shaped curve, with most data points near the center and fewer near the edges.

We say the point of inflection is "one standard deviation" from the center. This distance is called "Sigma".

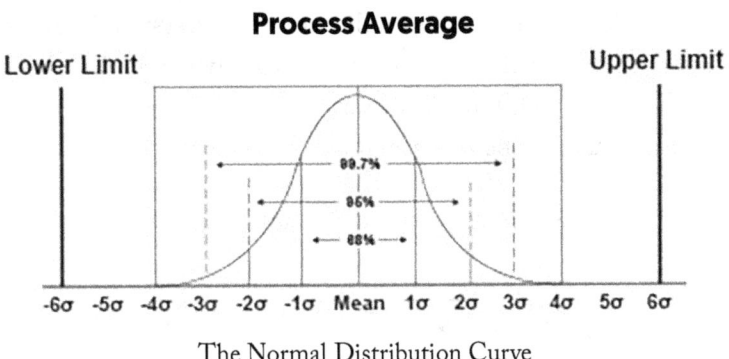

The Normal Distribution Curve

Normal Distribution tables signify where points are likely to occur. In our marble drop, most fell near the X, with fewer at the edges. A "Normal" distribution chart shows this quite well.

The popular Normal Curve describes many real-life examples with neat math properties. Using it, we can make strong predictions about how data points occur in real processes by using the Normal. If we know the parameters of a stable process, such as the Average (Mean) and Standard Deviation (spread), then observations outside 3-sigma limits are unlikely. We can say, with some confidence, that points *outside* the limits are due to *special* causes. In those cases, take Action!

However, data points *inside* these limits are due to *common* causes beyond our control. LEAVE THEM BE! Any attempt to adjust a stable process (tampering) always results in greater variation.

Understanding variation helps us work smarter. The only way *common* cause variations can be reduced is by a change in the *process*. In manufacturing and business, Management would be responsible for that. This is a smart division of labor:

Common Cause = Management Control, Special Cause = Worker Control. And this is the ONLY way it will work!

Let's look at another example, take a stable system (Harry's performance in a cleaning process at work which he has done for many months). This next chart measures the particle count present (smaller is better) each day after Harry's efforts.

Consequences of Misunderstanding Variation

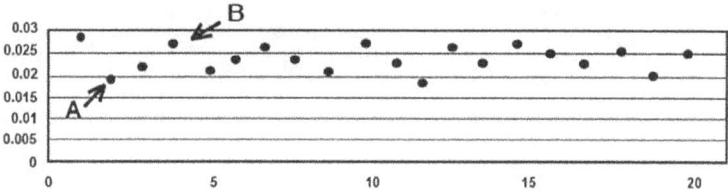

John, Harry's supervisor, sees the particle count fall, as shown on Day marked A. So John gives Harry some kudos! But it then gets worse (higher, see point B). So John kicks a little tush, and the performance improves. What kind of supervisor does John become? What works best, Kudos or Tush? John's approach is a formula for *increased* variation of results, not a decrease. John will exhaust himself trying to control the uncontrollable and Harry will feel unnecessarily micromanaged.

These examples illustrate the frustration when all variation is blamed on a single incorrect cause. The horizontal position of the funnel was not the cause of the variation, and John's verbal input was not the cause of Harry's success or failure. In both cases, proper data analysis was missed to identify the actual variation causes.

In summary:

1. Variation has two types of causes:

   a) Common Causes: Those inherently part of reprocessing that contribute to relatively small, apparently random shifts in outcomes hour after hour, day after day.
   b) Special Causes: Factors that drive the variation above the inherent in the system, arising because of special; circumstances.

Common cause variation is difficult, if not impossible, to link to any particular source. Special cause variation is called "assignable" because it can be tracked down to an identifiable source.

2. An economic balance must be found to minimize the negative impact of unnecessary intervention. We err when we:

   a) Look for assignable causes when they do not exist.
   b) Overlook assignable causes when they do exist.

The funnel example powerfully illustrates how missing the information in variation can sabotage even the best efforts, and it can lead to misunderstandings and useless course-corrections. If you are a supervisor working with a team, consider the problems that could arise from drawing these kinds of conclusions:

> "You've done it once; that proves you can do it every time."
> "You must perform above average all the time."

The lesson here is this: We must allow for variation in the performance of others, and ourselves. We all have a natural rhythm in our effectiveness and can expect improvement after an "off" day or two without meddling. Cutting each other and ourselves some slack can improve our psyche, strengthen key relationships, and yield better results.

3. A stable process (one with only common causes present) is said to be in a state of statistical control. The cause system for variation remains constant over time. In Statistical Control, variation in outcomes is *predictable* within statistically established limits. Knowing this, managers/supervisors can:

   a) Avoid blaming people for problems beyond their control.
   b) Avoid spending money on new equipment not needed.
   c) Avoid wasting time looking for causes for trends when nothing has changed.

Fun-Ditty #1.1

"There is nothing so useless as doing efficiently that which should not be done at all."
— Peter F. Drucker

1.2 — The Flow

During this period in Milwaukee, I sought better ways to teach the technology of instrumentation. Prompted by adult-student struggles, I developed ways to make learning the subject more enjoyable. In the process, I discovered that an essential principle in the art of instrumentation could be extrapolated from the study of "flow," which is observing the rate or quantity that liquids, gasses, or vapors pass through a measurable space.

Doing this requires three steps:

1) Measuring the flow
2) Comparing the measured flow with what is desired, and
3) Making corrections to bring the Measured flow value to the Desired value.

It is a fundamental concept, but this 3-step process underlies all instrumentation in technology: measurement, comparison, and correction. Applying the same principle to life goals can also help a person yield better career, relationship, or health results.

Often people fail to analyze their results to see how they measure up to what is desired and then systematically make proper course corrections until their desired outcome is realized. A closer look at the measure of flow in instrumentation reveals an even deeper principle that can help this be accomplished in life:

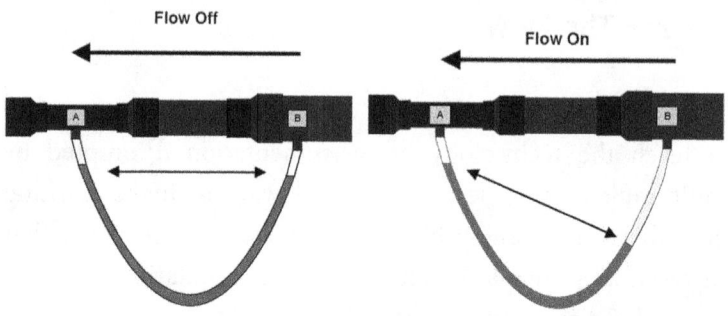

Here is a tube with varying diameters, A and B. Gas moves through the tube when the flow is ON. In my role as an educator, I asked my students the question:

"In what section will the pressure be highest,
A or B, when the flow is turned on?"

Invariably, the responses collectively pointed toward pressure being highest in the smallest part of the tube. After all, that seemed the most logical. Who hasn't put their thumb over a garden hose to increase the pressure of the water coming out? Doesn't a smaller opening cause faster flow and increased pressure? The students were surprised to discover that the opposite was the case. Faster flow corresponds instead to *lower* pressure.

The students discovered this when observing the small Venturi tube pictured here between points A and B containing colored liquid. They could see that as long as the flow was turned off, the pressure was equal between the smaller and larger segments of the tube. But when the flow was turned on, the pressure was higher in the larger tube, not the smaller one.

How can this be?

Think back to the garden hose. It makes more sense when you realize that *more* pressure is behind your thumb than in the water shooting through the air.

Lower pressure in the smaller tube results from the kinetic energy (energy possessed by the gas in motion) found there. When the kinetic energy increases with the gas flowing at a greater speed, pressure *decreases*, as shown by the changed level in the second figure.

To punch this principle home, I placed a standard air conditioner fan near the door of the lab in position to blow straight up, with a beach ball resting on the fan.

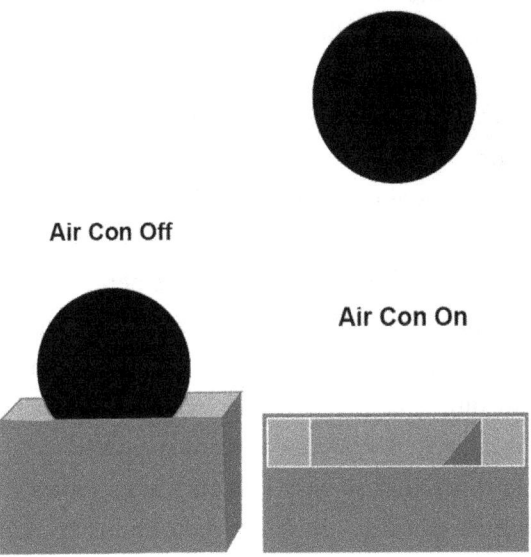

Position of the beach ball with the fan off and on.

Reason suggests the ball will blow away when the AC is turned on, but Viola! It merely hovers in place, as shown in the illustration.

What is remarkable is that the ball remains *in* the flow, even if we punch it out of the flow. It is pulled right back where the pressure is *least* (we call that a vacuum).

Nothing gets student attention quite like this when asked to explain why the ball pops back *into* the flow. Others come into the lab just to see this phenomenon. My students are happy to explain. This phenomenon is present in carburetors that inject gas into car engines. It is also why a twister or cyclone sucks houses and cars into its center.

The air moving up from the AC unit moves *faster* than the air around it. Faster air means *lower* pressure. Slower air outside the blowing AC stream was *higher* pressure, acting as a wall to keep the ball in the middle of the stream. Physics affirms that an object will flow in the path of *least* resistance, so in this case, gravity acting upon the ball causes it to fall and rest where the air pressure is *lowest*, namely *inside* the speeding stream of air.

This phenomenon is so counter-intuitive that it never fails to captivate. But what is truly unique is how we can apply this principle to life. When we're feeling tremendous amounts of pressure in life, it's often because we spend more time thinking about our responsibilities than putting ourselves in motion to carry them out. Pressure is higher where movement is slow. Pressure is alleviated when movement speeds up.

People think that staying in a forward motion with their responsibilities can directly affect their ability to manage the many pressures of life. But it does more than that. Like a ball resting easily and balancing perfectly on the AC flow, we can experience more ease and greater balance by simply staying in a steady flow of activity toward our desired objectives.

Staying in *motion* provides the increase of kinetic energy that, by law, results in lower pressure. The feeling of being in balance and at greater ease can be experienced immediately. When you feel stress or tension, rather than contemplating all the reasons you are overburdened, *do* something. *Move.* Make the phone call. File the paperwork. Increase your kinetic energy, and the pressure must immediately drop. Every time you stew and worry, your kinetic energy goes down, and by the laws of physics, the stress you feel will go *up*.

It doesn't mean you must always be doing something or constantly moving. It simply means you now have conscious control over how much pressure or stress you choose to suffer. As you apply this principle, you'll find an unseen force like the wall of air next to the AC stream that can hold everything in place for you while you operate "in the flow."

Learning to operate in the FLOW is one of the first of many more secrets to come.

Fun-Ditty #1.2

> *"Laughter is the closest thing to the grace of God."*
> *- Karl Barth*

1.3 — Honeywell – MOL – from Milwaukee to California - Mind Model

Prompted by salary concerns, I left education to work again in aerospace. I trained for six months at Honeywell in Minneapolis on a guidance & control system. Then we moved to California as technical support for the Air Force space program, the Manned Orbiting Laboratory (MOL).

The MOL was part of the United States Air Force's human spaceflight program. MOL evolved into a single-use laboratory, for which crews would be launched on 40-day missions, then returned to earth using a vehicle derived from NASA's Gemini spacecraft.

The program was announced on December 10th, 1963, as a habitable platform to prove the usefulness of putting people into space for military missions. Astronauts selected were told later about the secret mission. The prime contractor was McDonnell Aircraft and the laboratory was built by the Douglas Aircraft Company. Honeywell provided guidance and control (G&C). (https://en.wikipedia.org/wiki/Manned_Orbiting_Laboratory)

Manned Orbiting Laboratory (MOL)

The MOL never reached fruition, but much work was accomplished before being canceled in June 1969. During the

1960s, the MOL had been competing with the Vietnam War for funds, and budget cuts repeatedly postponed its first flight. A single unmanned test flight of the Gemini B spacecraft was conducted on November 3rd, 1966, but the test flight of the MOL was canceled in June 1969, as was my service on the MOL.

To keep from going under, I began working in a training business with a man by the name of Al Tomsik who spoke fluent Japanese and had served as a Japanese interpreter/interrogator during the 2nd World War. According to him, the U.S. government told the Japanese they were going to drop the atomic bomb. Their response was "Mokasatsu" – a Japanese word with two connotations:

1) We decline with contempt, or
2) We defer until further consideration.

A great lesson to show that words can kill, and that the pen is mightier than the sword.

It was in the early seventies when I worked with Al. His was a business promoting good ideas and concepts that would lead to success in any venture. He was a good member of the church and the wealth and understanding he had at his fingertips was impressive, though my endeavors in that venture only yielded me $400 in four months.

While I worked with Al, he introduced me to the stickman, or Mind Model by Dr. Thurman Fleet, founder of Concept Therapy. I didn't use it in the 70's, but he used it when I worked for him and I never forgot it. I would use the concepts later to help students in trainings of my own.

Al shared with me the following notes, which he had captured in his studies with Fleet, adding a comment directly for me. As I was still early in my career, he impressed upon my mind this one point above the others. He said, "You can do anything you want, but understand this. If you don't know how this works, you haven't got a snowball's chance of doing it." It made a lasting impact.

Dr. Thurman Fleet in the 1930's, in San Antonio, Texas, as related to me by Al Tomsik:

> "You are going to have to alter some ideas in your mind, but in order to do that, you are going to have to have a picture to work with, and he told me about a doctor in San Antonio, Texas who started the Concept Therapy movement, who was trying to teach the healing arts and he ran into a problem. He said the medical profession, of which he was a member, were treating symptoms for effects, they were not treating causes. But if you are ever going to enjoy whole health, you must treat the whole person. That's called Holistic healing. He said if we're going to treat the whole person, we're going to have to give them a picture of the other side of their personality. And he said, "Since no person has ever seen the mind, I'm going to make a picture of the mind."
>
> He said, "Let this represent the mind. And then let this represent, what we've given all of our total attention to up to now, the

body. You see, the body is what provides the action that produces our results. To change our results, we must change our actions. But our actions are driven by the mind. If we're going to change what's going on in the mind, we're going to have to understand how it functions. And as he pointed out, there are two sections to the mind. Joined together, but different in their method of operation. He called this the conscious mind and this the sub-conscious mind. What we have here is a picture to begin to work with.

In his illustrations, Dr. Thurman Fleet gave us a powerful clue to our minds. Using a simple picture he explained how our mind works. He said the medical profession, of which he was a member, was treating symptoms for effects, not treating causes.

He said if we treat the whole person, we must give them a picture of the other side of their personality. And he said, "since no person has ever seen the mind, I'm going to take a picture of the mind. Let this represent the MIND."

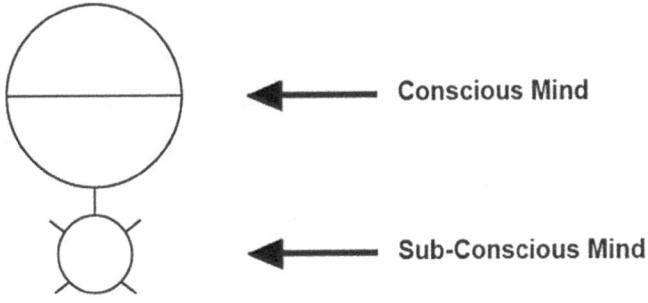

There are two sections to the mind, joined together, but different in how they operate. Dr. Fleet called the top the conscious mind and the bottom sub-conscious mind.

He continued, "And then let this represent what we've given all of our total attention to up to now, the BODY."

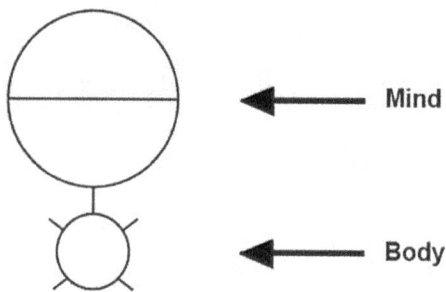

"You see, the body is what provides the action that produces our results. To change our results, we must change our actions. But our actions are driven by the mind."

He explained that the top is the part of us that thinks, reasons, and our free will lies here. The Conscious mind can accept or reject any idea. No person or circumstance can cause us to think about thoughts or ideas we do not choose.

He went on to explain that the "thoughts" we choose eventually determine our results. All pain, pleasure, and limitation are held in the Conscious mind. But as we accept a thought, it is impressed upon the second part of our mind.

It is the most magnificent part, the power center. It works in every cell of our body. Each thought our conscious mind chooses to accept, this part must accept! It cannot reject!

All thoughts impressed upon the Sub-Conscious, over and over, become fixed in this part. Fixed ideas then continue with no conscious assistance until they are replaced. We call these fixed ideas Habits.

The Body, the smallest part, is our physique. It is merely the instrument of our mind, or the house in which we live. Our thoughts drive our actions; our actions determine our results. In other words, the process for creating change flows through the following steps:

1. Thoughts, 2. Feelings, 3. Actions, 4. Results!

Dr. Fleet also explained that when one desires to be an individual, expressing uniqueness in the face of all criticism, the masses try to hold them back. They criticize, ridicule, and condemn them. He added, "They've even crucified them." So what do these individuals have to do? They have to move to the next level of conscious awareness, and they have to develop discipline.

A lot of people view discipline as punishment. But Fleet says discipline is simply when we can give ourselves a command and follow it. As we bring discipline into our life, our world starts to change.

Learning is when we consciously entertain a new idea, get emotionally involved in the idea, step out and act on the idea, and change the results. It's the experience from the change in results that is the learning experience. He quoted Eric Hoffman, who said, "In times of change, the learners will inherit the earth while the learned find themselves beautifully equipped to deal with a world that no longer exists."

We must keep learning, and if we do, we will move to the point of mastery. You eliminate competition when you do that. You develop a strength that is called confidence. Fleet thinks of confidence as strength with style. It's when you know, and you know that you know. It's a beautiful thing, when you are giving everything you've got, and love it.

Al's notes also included the wisdom of Wallace D. Wattles who taught:

> We say know the truth, and the truth will set you free. I think you've heard that before. Well, there is only one thing to be free of, and that is ignorance. And you know there is only one way to get rid of ignorance. And that's through knowledge. And there is only one way to get to knowledge, and that's through knowledge. And that's what you are doing right now. To think what you want to think is to think truth, regardless of appearance, according to Wallace D. Wattles.
>
> Wallace also said, "Calmness of mind is one of the beautiful jewels of wisdom. It is the result of long and patient effort in self-control. Its presence indicates ripened experience and a more than ordinary knowledge of the laws and operations of thought.
>
> "A person becomes calm in the measure that they understand themselves as a thought-evolved being, for such knowledge necessitates understanding others as the result of thought. And as he develops a right understanding and sees more clearly, the internal relations of things by the action of cause and effect, he ceases the thought of worry and greed, and he remains poised, steadfast, and serene." (Wattles, Wallace D. The Science of Getting Rich. Holyoake, Mass., 1910.)

Though the wisdom was profound and seeds were planted, it would be some time before those seeds would bear fruit. With my wife four months pregnant with our fourth child, I wrote in my journal:

> *9/1/70 Waited in line 2 hours at the welfare office, only to find that I was not eligible for financial assistance since I was self-employed, i.e. Tomsik. Still may be eligible for medical, but must go back to Santa Ana office. Had lunch, decided to lay myself off, returned to welfare office. But they had closed for the day...*

I did not know it yet, but my career was about to move me through some experiences that would teach me the interconnectedness of true, universal principles that can be applied to succeed in industry, business, and life. One of those principles is striking the proper balance between analysis and judgment.

We do our best to make decisions based on sound, measurable data. For example, if I am to take a new job or position, it will only be after weighing out the pros and cons, and calculating the advantages and disadvantages both monetarily and psychologically. But even after the balance sheet is complete, the decision still comes down to a judgment call. Sometimes the numbers don't support the gut instinct or spiritual impression about a matter, and those unmeasurable factors necessarily do have an impact.

As Alain C. Enthoven explained, "Ultimately all policies [or decisions] are made based on judgments. There is no other way, and there never will be. The question is whether those judgments have to be made in the fog of inadequate and inaccurate data, unclear and undefined issues, and a welter of conflicting personal opinions, or whether they can be made on the basis of adequate, reliable information, relevant experience, and clearly drawn issues. In the end, analysis is but an aid to judgment. Judgment is supreme." Alain C. Enthoven, Business Week, Nov. 1965.

And this situation we found ourselves proved to be no different. A friend, Errol Greenleaf, got me a job selling TV's at Sears in Long Beach for a while, but it was time to use our best judgment and make some new decisions.

> "We shall have to evolve
> Problem solvers galore
> Since each problem they solve
> Creates ten problems more!"
> - Piet Hein

> "You must tear down the old
> to build the new."
> - K. Sekine

Fun-Ditty #1.3

> *"Nothing fails like success because we don't learn from it. We learn only from failure."*
> *- Kenneth Boulding*

1.4 — Determination

After my termination from the MOL, and after I had to lay myself off from the training company, I found jobs repairing

TVs, loading freight, and delivering newspapers. Eventually I gratefully accepted a teaching position in a high school, spending the next eight years in secondary education, first for a short stint in Moab, Utah and then on to a larger school in Orem about a four hour drive to the northwest.

While teaching at Orem High School in 1974, I worked with my students to build a radio tower and establish KOHS, a station licensed by the Federal Communications Commission and run by students. At the time I wrote this, it was still in operation five decades later. This turn of events strengthened my love for teaching, despite the low teacher wages.

OHS Radio Station Begins Broadcasting

On Friday, November 1st, over a year of planning will become a reality when Orem High School's radio station KOHS begins broadcasting.

"We have the best broadcasting facilities in the area," says Mr. Brian Pead, teacher at Orem High and future Program Manager at the radio station.

"Our goal at the present time, Mr. Pead says, "is to graduate from Orem High eight students per year who will be qualified immediately to work in sales, production, news, programming, music selection (soft rock), and publicity promotion. In three years, when the station is in full swing, we plan to graduate six to ten students who will have first-class radio-telephone licenses."

"To give the students the needed training and experience, KOHS will be totally student-operated, with faculty supervision. From 7 a.m. until 5 p.m. student disc jockeys will be broadcasting soft rock, school and public announcements, and school atheletic events. Play-by-play also will eventually be given by students.

Twenty-five students will also be involved in the electronics and maintenance area of the station, under the supervision of Mr. Bob E. Robertson, Chief Engineer, who originated the idea of KOHS.

After the initial installation, the operating budget for the station is expected to be $1,000 to $1,500. The station will have a range of twenty miles "line of sight."

"We would appreciate the support of the community," says Mr. Pead. "We welcome their public announcements and want to be of service to the community. Address public announcements to Brian Pead, Orem High School.

While so engaged, I pursued a master's degree in Industrial Education and published the electronics text for Prentice-hall ("Essentials of Semiconductor Circuits" 1976). While teaching high school electronics, a job I loved, I found the following quote:

"It strikes me dumb to look over the long series of faces, such as any full church, courthouse, London tavern meeting, or miscellany of men will show them. Some score or two of years ago, all these were little red-colored infants; each of them capable of being kneaded, baked into any social form you choose; yet see now how they are fixed and hardened – into artists, artisans, clergy, gentry, learned sergeants, unlearned

dandies, and can and shall now be nothing else hence-forth."
Thomas Carlyle

I wrote in my journal dated 1979: "If the above is true, life is over for me. I don't want life to be over for me. I must now look at my life. Set it in order to become what I want. I am 42, half through (God willing). But of greatest import is the idea that no one else cares what I become. Therefore, I can let no one else determine what I will be. It is my ball game. It is time to act, not react...."

Fun-Ditty #1.4a

> "Lincoln was not great because he was born in a log cabin, but because he got out of it."
> – James Truslow Adams

Fun-Ditty #1.4b

> "Find a purpose in life so big it will challenge every capacity to be at your best."
> – David O. McKay

1.5 — The Wisdom of Deming

Secondary-Ed at the high school allowed me to engage in off-campus activities. While working evenings on the master's degree, I also worked weekends and summers at a local factory, Signetics Corp. This role gave me excellent savvy in the integrated circuit assembly process.

After seven years at the school and needing a better income to support my wife and four children, I accepted a position at Signetics as a Maintenance Manager, learning about the issues the company struggled with to make money. I was introduced to the moniker "Good-Cheap-Fast," as the key to survival that made a lot of sense. The product must meet the spec (Good), it must be delivered at a cost that will attract customers (Cheap), and it must be delivered on time (Fast). As a management team member, I shared in several drives to improve the quality (Good-Cheap-Fast) bottom line.

William Edwards Deming was an American statistician, college professor, author, lecturer, and consultant, noted for improving production in the US during World War II. Signetics employed a quality guru to teach us Deming's principles. During the first of several sessions, it was clear Deming was different. There was no talk of inspection, a key element to what we knew as quality.

Quality had been a system of inspecting the final product to know when to adjust the machine(s). Deming thought this view was incorrect. If quality is built-in rather than inspected, then quality is a management function. Not a function of the workforce!

In those first sessions, the Deming model destroyed my notions of management. We learned the important things we'd been taught were wrong. Not only were they wrong, but they led to poor quality, unhappy customers, and an unhappy workforce.

The leader asked, "When is a firm getting the best quality from its people?" One of our group responded, "I think people have to be happy for there to be quality." That response was a thundering wake-up to our group! That it came from our group magnified its impact. The leader responded, "Not a bad answer. Quality is pride of workmanship."

It was a radical concept at the time, that success follows happiness, not the other way around.

Deming listed problems with the quality effort, saying an emphasis on short-term profit lands at the top. (I've included a more complete overview of his principles in the Notes for this chapter.)

The principles he taught can be illustrated with a graphic he called the Red Bead exercise, where he scooped a paddle with 50 slots into a bucket with red and white beads. The bead bucket had 10% red beads and 90% white. A scoop with holes drilled part-way into the board collected red and white beads with each scoop. The objective was to reach in and scoop out only white beads.

Deming enlisted class members to try their hand with scoops but found they could not get only white beads. He posed the question, "Will punishing the operators (bead scoopers) for getting red beads improve the Bead Scoop process?" As it became clear that this approach would be fruitless, he taught, "Don't just do the same things better – find better things to do."

Then if it is not the role of Quality Control to punish workers for poor performance, what is its role? The role of QC is instead to merely operate as "tasters." That is, to understand the customers' taste, and know what's acceptable.

For example, if a business is about baking cakes, QC operates as the taster. However, if the company implements too tight of a taste test without knowing the customer's preference, you may inadvertently scrap a product that your customer would be happy with.

To illustrate this further, a firm wanted to make the world's best dog food. It used the latest animal nutrition, made in spotless automatic kitchens, packaged so that it would jump off the supermarket shelves into the shopping cart. Award-winning commercials supported it.

The product took off, then died. An international marketing consultant was brought in to see what went wrong. When he returned with his report, it simply said, "The dogs don't like it!" What does this tell us about producing quality? They were following the faulty "good, cheap, fast" approach.

Instead, let's listen, care, risk, and have fun.

The implications of this principle are vast. Imagine what would happen if we followed this principle, not just in manufacturing, but in life? How would relationships, for example, improve by listening more, caring about what the other person wants, taking more risks, and having fun? It's important to shift from a focus on short-term wins to longer-term success. Yes, the Deming Secret can be applied to other areas of life besides manufacturing.

Fun-Ditty #1.5

"One of the best ways to persuade others is with your ears – by listening to them."

– Dean Rusk

NOTES FOR CHAPTER 1

Additional thoughts related to this chapter:

Broaden Your View

Following are some brain teasers and notes that I shared with students to get them thinking. I begin this section with the idea of "Smart-Think," to broaden our view of problems and procedures we bump into daily. Each time, the issue is our "mindset" concerning the world around us.

Consider the following puzzle to broaden your outlook: Arrange the six toothpicks to form four identical triangles.

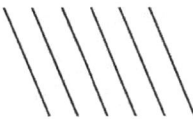 Arrange the six toothpicks to form four identical triangles.

Stumped? Try forming them in 3-dimensional space.

Tips for Problem-Solving

When you have a problem, you can write a challenge statement, study it for a while, then leave it, change it, stretch and squeeze it, and restate it until you feel the challenge is centered, then you are ready.

- Write the problem as a definite question, beginning with "In what way might I...?
- Vary the wording of the challenge by substituting synonyms for keywords.
- Stretch the challenge to see the broader perspective.
- Squeeze the challenge to see the narrow perspective.
- Divide it into sub-problems.
- Solve the sub-problems.
- Keep asking, "how else?" and "why else?"

The Man in the Beans

I brought my students some relief from the technical side with an exercise many will enjoy. I asked my class members to raise a hand when they found the man in the beans. It says something about the way our mind is more dominant, Left or Right. Some find it immediately; others struggle. Google "Man in the Beans" to try the exercise for yourself. The point: We're not all put together the same, and that's ok, neither good nor bad

Additional notes from William Edwards Deming's work

Deming offered fourteen fundamental principles for management to follow to improve their business. The points were first presented in his famous book "Out of the Crisis." Below is a condensation of his 14 Points for Management:

> Rule #1 – Create constancy of purpose; plan for quality in the long term.
>
> Rule #2 – Embrace quality throughout the organization. Create your quality vision, and implement it.
>
> Rule #3 – Inspections are costly and unreliable – and they don't improve quality; they merely find a lack of quality.
>
> Rule #4 – End the practice of awarding business on price alone: instead, minimize total cost by working with a single supplier: Look at suppliers as your partners in quality. Encourage them to spend time improving their own quality.

Rule #5 – Improve constantly every process for planning, production, and service: to improve quality and productivity and thus decrease costs.

Rule #6 – Institute training on the job: build a foundation of common knowledge. Allow workers to understand their roles in the "big picture."

Rule #7 – Adopt and institute leadership: Don't simply supervise – provide support and resources so that each staff member can do his or her best. Be a coach instead of a policeman.

Rule #8 – Drive out fear: Allow people to perform at their best by ensuring that they're not afraid to express ideas or concerns. Make workers feel valued and encourage them to look for better ways to do things.

Rule #9 – Break down barriers between staff areas: People in research, design, sales, and production must work as a team to foresee problems and avoid them.

Rule #10 – Eliminate slogans for the workforce: Let people know exactly what you want – don't make them guess. Don't let words and nice-sounding phrases replace effective leadership.

Rule #11 – Eliminate numerical quotas for the workforce and numerical goals for management: Look at *how* the process is carried out, not just numerical targets. Measure the *process* rather than the people behind the process.

> Rule #12 – Remove barriers that rob people of pride in workmanship and eliminate the annual rating or merit system.
>
> Rule #13 – Institute a vigorous program of education and self-improvement for everyone: Improve the current skills of workers. Encourage people to learn new skills to prepare for future changes and challenges.
>
> Rule #14 – Put everybody in the company to work accomplishing the transformation: The transformation is everybody's job. Improve your overall organization by having each person take a step toward quality.

It was a very long list for a manager to consider, but success would only come with everyone on board – from the on-line worker to the company president. That was the genius of W. Edwards Deming.

Deming placed quality in two main groups:

1) Features
2) Freedom from defects

He asserted that 85% of the reasons for failure were deficiencies in the process rather than the employee. Management's role was to change the process rather than badgering individuals to do better. Two important elements were at the root of all issues:

a) Journey from symptom to cause is the diagnostic.
b) Cause to the fix is remedial and much easier.

A problem many face is confusing the symptom with the cause of the rejection or problem. We in America have worried about specifications, focused on meeting the spec, and sounding the alarm when a spec is not met.

We've learned to live in a world of mistakes and defective products as if they were necessary for life. It is time we adopt a new philosophy in America.

Some of my favorite Deming Truisms include:

- 'Rational behavior requires theory. Reactive behavior requires only reflex action."
- "If you can't describe what you are doing as a process, you don't know what you are doing."
- "You should not ask questions without knowledge."
- "The result of long-term relationships is better and better quality and lower and lower costs."
- "Profit in business comes from repeat customers, customers who boast about your product or service and bring friends with them."
- "We've learned to live in a world of mistakes and defective products as if they were necessary. It is time we adopt a new philosophy in America."
- "Eighty-five percent of the reasons for failure are deficiencies in the systems and process rather than the employee. The role of management is to change the process rather than badgering individuals to do better."
- "Don't just do the same things better – find better things to do."

I was stunned by Deming's wisdom. He went on to highlight Seven Deadly Diseases and Obstacles:

1. Lack of constancy of purpose, planning products that will have a market, keeping the company in business, and providing jobs.
2. Emphasis on short-term profits (just the opposite from constancy of purpose to stay in business).
3. Evaluation of performance, merit rating, or annual review.
4. Mobility of management; job-hopping.
5. Management using only visible figures, with little or no consideration of unknown figures.

6. Excessive medical costs
7. Excessive costs of liability, swelled by lawyers working on contingency fees.

Deming went to Japan first and taught the math of CONTROL; he then told the Japanese they needed to talk to his friend Juran, who taught IMPROVEMENT (the management side of the coin). Juran published his Quality Control Handbook in 1951, which the Japanese got hold of and asked, who is Juran? We'll see more about Juran later.

CHAPTER 2

Singapore

2.0 – Willingness to Pivot

In the Official Naval Institute magazine, Frank Cope described an experience at sea where a battleship was navigating through stormy weather. The lookout noticed a light in the distance, so he alerted the captain who asked whether it was steady or moving.

The lookout replied, "Steady, captain," which meant they were on a dangerous collision course with the other ship.

So the captain replied, "Advise the ship to change course 20 degrees."

The signal was sent, but a signal came back, "Advisable for you to change course 20 degrees."

He countered, "I'm a captain; change course 20 degrees."

To his surprise, the reply came, "I'm a seaman second class, change your course 20 degrees."

The captain grew increasingly furious and barked his threat, "I'm a battleship. Change YOUR course," to which it replied: "I'm a lighthouse. Your call."

In that moment, the captain experienced a paradigm shift, and changed his course.

There comes a time when life requires not only a change of perspective, but sometimes also unexpected course corrections. Though I was learning new skills and gaining valuable experience in my career in the States, I was about to experience a seismic paradigm shift and the need (or opportunity) to move in a new direction.

It was 1979 in Utah, early in my career, when I worked for a group called RONHIC (Ready Or Not, Here I Come), a division of a company called Zylotec. I worked part-time, helping to prepare a training course on micro-computers. The training course was for industrial customers, training their employees to use this new technological breakthrough to do many things faster and better.

I had only recently been bitten by the computer bug (during the spring and summer of the previous year), and when I got involved with this group in about November, I thought this was it. And so I thrust my heart and soul into the effort. I had been working part-time and full-time all summer for Signetics since about November 1977 but slowly phased it out with my activity in RONHIC.

I spent one week in Albuquerque, New Mexico, on a trip financed by RONHIC. The trip down was unreal. Our team got caught in a snowstorm, driving a camper, and the drive shaft broke and fell off on a little hill at about midnight. We got the camper off the road and bedded down for the night.

The following day we found ourselves snowed in somewhere in the middle of the Navajo reservation. We finally got a ride from a Navajo man in a pickup to the nearest trading post, where we called for a wrecker from Gallup. We left the camper in Gallup for work and took a bus to Albuquerque, where we spent the week taking a course in microprocessors by WINTEK, which was a great learning experience.

Things looked better and better with RONHIC. I began to consider taking a Sabbatical from Orem High School to spend a year with RONHIC full-time. As we got into the development of our microprocessor training course, it became evident there were some real problems among the management as to what they wanted. The project fell apart.

Since I had already applied for the sabbatical at the high school, I approached Signetics for a possible full-time position. I was offered a position as a maintenance supervisor in the assembly area. I accepted the job and began full-time with Signetics in June 1979, working on line maintenance and supervising eleven technicians. We maintained all equipment in the assembly area, where the tiny integrated circuits were put together. I became like a father to the techs. I'd given up my role as an instructor in the high school but found much the same feeling at Signetics; these guys were my students. I was older than all of them.

We organized the group in a fine manner and provided better maintenance support than in the past, receiving praise for our efforts. The financial rewards were good, providing close to what I made at the school and what I had been earning part-time at Signetics. With my new position, it was a new and neat experience being home each evening with the family.

I spent a lot of time helping Valerie with her math assignments. She would try hard. The sessions would often end in tears, but she would stay with it and do very well. I received many satisfying hours with my work both at home and in Line Maintenance.

After I started with Signetics, I was on a trip to Boston for a week to train on a machine we used, made by a company called Mech-el industries. The plane flew from Salt Lake to Kansas City on the first leg.

As we flew out of Salt Lake, it was a clear day, and I was fascinated by the terrain below, especially the Wasatch/Uintah mountains. It was like I was looking at a neat topographical map. When I was in the 4th grade, my family moved into a home in Moab, and in the attic, there were stacks of old National Geographic magazines. I would lay and study the maps for hours in the attic, fantasizing about traveling and seeing all the places with weird names. As I read the maps' titles, I would pronounce them in my mind the way they should sound. It came as quite a shock in later years to find that most adults and even some newscasters didn't know how to pronounce many of those names correctly!

As we crossed part of the high Uintahs, I could see dozens and dozens of tiny lakes, many with snow still down to the water. I remember my dad talking of the Granddaddy Lakes in the Uintah, where he served with the Civilian Conservation Corps (CCCs) during the depression. As I looked, I thought about getting some good maps of the area and hiking into them with our son. That could be one of our things. It shouldn't be too hard to get into it. Then I thought, but what of the girls? Leslie would especially want to go. We could handle that, but we better start small and work up.

Back on the flight, I sat next to a nice young gentleman from Boston on the trip's second leg. His name was John Peters, and he had been to a convention in Denver. We talked of life, Boston, his business, etc. We got on very well, and he invited me to dinner with his wife one night while I was in Boston. He and his gracious wife, Wendy, took me to an old restaurant in downtown Boston called Durgin-Park, established in the 1700s. With the help of a kind old lady at the next table, I had my first lobster, got that nasty shell off, and enjoyed the meat. It was a wonderful evening.

I worked in Line Maintenance at Signetics in Utah for six months, then was promoted to engineering, where I became a Senior Hermetic Assembly Engineer. After a year in engineering, where I had a super job with great associates and experiences, my wife was still working in the billing office at the local hospital. It seemed like we weren't getting anywhere financially, unable to get our old debts paid. I had a business trip to Sunnyvale, California, in about August and answered some help-wanted ads in the local paper while there. There seemed to be some good opportunities in the area, but living costs would wipe out any salary gains. Not too promising. But a bridge was crossed in the mental decision to look elsewhere for a better job, even though I loved the job at Signetics. My paradigm began to shift.

In October, one of the techs who worked for me, Steve Killpack, got a call from a head-hunter saying he had a job as Sales Manager for Mech-El (mentioned previously). Steve publicly announced in the office what the caller had offered. I was interested, so I called Carl Roberts, who had been the Corporate Engineering Manager for Signetics in Sunnyvale, California. I had known him from his days at Signetics, but he had quit and gone to work for Mech-El some four months earlier. After the phone call, my wife and I were on our way to Boston to discuss the possibility of going to Singapore for three years. An offer was made, and we accepted!!!

It was 1982, and I was to work with my colleagues in Singapore, setting up a field-service office for Mech-El Industries, a company trying to sell a new automatic wire bonder to Intel. My wife and four children supported me in this move across the Pacific as I pursued this endeavor. A new field service operation was required before Intel would be interested in the new bonder. I was to direct that office.

Where is Singapore?

Singapore is a small island-country in Southeast Asia, at the tip of the Malaysian peninsula.

After giving my two weeks' notice, I was through with Signetics in Utah. I spent a week in Boston, Massachusetts for more training and a few days in Portland, Maine on a machine installation for Mech-El. I then spent two weeks installing a machine of all places at Signetics. I spent Thanksgiving with family while there, and then I was off to Manteca, California, to install two Mech-El devices. We scheduled our move to Singapore for January 7th.

SINGAPORE

I got home from California on Wednesday afternoon, Christmas Eve, and had a delightful Christmas with my family. We didn't have a tree since all the tree stuff was packed, so we all went to Grandma Fay's new condo apartment for breakfast. She gave our son an 8mm rifle which his Grandad Wesley had assembled and built a stock with our son in mind before he died. Fay had waited until he was older to give it to him. There couldn't have been a neater gift in the world for him.

We took a few trips to the rifle range and had a good time. Then after some packing and moving, I headed for the airport to return to Boston for two days to organize myself on Sunday. I ran into the fog at the point of the mountain and waited all day for it to lift so we could take off. After the last possible flight was canceled for the day with no fog relief in sight, I made arrangements for a strange itinerary—Pocatello to Twin Falls, Boise to Denver to Kansas City, and finally to Boston. I couldn't take the chance and not get out of Salt Lake on Monday. So I rented a car and drove to Pocatello, then found myself on my way to Boise on a two-motor prop job with two passengers and a crew of two.

I had seen a Norman Rockwell Post Magazine cover scene at the Pocatello airport that morning. A tall thin young man with boots, new Levi's, a black cowboy hat, and one suitcase was boarding a plane as his parents watched on. His dad had an old baseball cap on, a plaid farmer's jacket, and his irrigating boots on with the pant cuffs tucked in. His mom was a dear little squatty lady in old blue jeans and aspirations in her eyes. It would have been interesting to know the details of that story.

I transferred to Republic Airlines, flying to Denver from Boise with no trouble. I boarded TWA in Denver for a pleasant flight to Kansas City, where, would you believe, FOG! My flight to Boston was canceled as I spent the night in Kansas

City. I flew to Atlanta the following day, then to Washington DC, and on to Boston. I arrived Tuesday night at 8:30 after leaving Orem, Utah, on Sunday morning. What a trip.

I had an excellent visit at Mech-El. I spent the next day, New Year's eve, at the plant, talking with the company leaders and getting paperwork ready for the big move. I finished in time to catch a flight out of Boston to Denver without a hitch, but as we got off the plane in Denver, the flight to Salt Lake was canceled, again due to fog! We were hustled onto a bus, where I spent the next eleven hours sitting next to a delightful Jewish fellow, Raphael Lewi, getting us to Salt Lake.

We talked through the night, arriving just before dawn in a thick fog. It was a fantastic experience talking with Raphael. He was born in Israel and was in the Israeli army when he was seventeen. He taught Hebrew in Arab refugee camps, came to Salt Lake to teach Educational Administration at the University of Utah, and became a specialist working for the Salt Lake School District. Speaking of the anticipated cultural shock we will experience in Singapore, he related the cultural shock he and his family experienced living in the Mormon community in Salt Lake.

I hoped to see him again. I gained a great insight into how a Jew feels about Jesus and, more specifically, about Mormons. Quite an eye-opener. I thought it would be good to write him a letter when we got to Singapore. Our visit on the bus and the resulting discussions strengthened my understanding of the art of conversation: to be a good conversationalist, all you need to do is ask questions and listen. As long as I could ask meaningful questions, the conversation flowed easily and kept Raphael interested.

While in Singapore, we sampled life among a variety of cultures. Native housing called kampongs included huddles of thatched huts, vegetable patches, and pigsties under a cover of coconut palms. All this was in the shadow of skyscrapers in the heart of modern Singapore.

A Kampong

Singapore Skyline

Our first reaction to Singapore was that it seemed a bit sterile, even repressive. But the crime rate was so low I didn't worry about my family. Then a friend drove into a traffic circle against the rules and got a computerized summons without seeing a live policeman. Big brother was watching.

Singapore's foreign minister once said, "This is a heavenly city for global corporations. For the corporate man or woman with a perk-fattened paycheck (Expats), life here can be easy and opulent, often monotonously so. Singapore is something of a gilded cage. Over 600 foreign manufacturers had chosen Singapore as their "export platform," setting up shop on industrial estates." *(Newman, Barry. East of the Equator. Hong Kong, Dow Jones Asia, 1980.)*

Before this opportunity to move to Singapore had come across my desk, I didn't even know what an expat was; now, I was one.

With the move overseas, my career was poised to soar. Our new life in Singapore promised to be both enchanting and profitable. However, it wouldn't be long before we would discover that, for us at least, it would be neither.

Fun-Ditty #2.0

> *"Never let your head hang down. Never give up and sit down and grieve. Find another way. And don't pray when it rains if you don't pray when the sun shines."*
>
> *- Satchel Paige*

CHAPTER 3

Indonesia

3.0 – Plot Twist

To make a very long story short, in 1981, I took that job and my young family overseas in Singapore with the promise of a three-year assignment. There, I learned what the term expat meant because now, finally, I was one.

However, after only four months in Singapore, Intel did not only NOT buy hundreds of our bonders, the field service office was summarily closed! With industry and business conditions in the turbulent 1980s, I was laid off. I had not been trained for this situation. There we were, my young family and I, without visible means of support in a foreign country. The company was willing to pay for our return, but we'd made too many sacrifices with the move. My wife and I with our children had already left our old life behind, renting our home to someone else, leaving schools, and leaving jobs; I didn't want to return to the states where we had already said our goodbyes and where I no longer had a job.

So instead, I hit the streets of Singapore. After several nail-biting weeks, I found a company with a factory in Jakarta, Indonesia, that was hiring. It was a one-hour flight south across the Equator. They made an offer, so I prepared to spend the next three years with my family as an Expat Engineering Manager with a semiconductor assembly factory called Fairchild Electronics.

To say I had been struggling was an understatement, but in this new position, I was about to discover yet another key to achieving success in industry and life. What I didn't realize at the time is that the hardships I had experienced (combined with the various training I had been receiving for twenty years prior) led me to this one grand adventure and the profound discoveries it had in store for me.

Fun-Ditty #3.0

"It is not the strongest of the species that survive, nor the most intelligent, but the one most responsive to change."

- Charles Darwin

3.1 — Perspective

Praise the Lord! We were headed to Jakarta, Indonesia, and I would be doing what I had done at Signetics in Utah before the move to Asia. By this time, our eldest daughter Marcie left us for her first year at the university stateside, so it was us remaining five, learning to adapt to the Muslim culture of Jakarta.

To get a flavor for what this transition was like, and the perspective it offered, here are some excerpts from a letter I sent to my mother describing the beginnings of our Indonesian expat experience:

> *Dear Mom, I'm sitting in our car, driven by our special driver, typing this note to you on a portable typewriter. This is better than worrying about all the cars we almost run into or cows that almost run into us. Typing this on my way home from work, about an hour both ways every day. Here it is 10 minutes later, having the typewriter thrown out of my lap three times, what with the bumps and grinds of a normal ride home. Almost the first paragraph of nonsense is completed. You probably think I'm drunk. Wish I were!*
>
> *As I was saying, to help you remember who this is, you've probably guessed by now, so why the charade, eh? Yes, it's Bob, number one son, speaking from downtown Jakarta, where the air is not so dry nor clean, but nonetheless palatable (there are some who would argue that point, but you can find those in every crowd)!*

Wow!...that was close. Nearing the halfway point, my driver is a little kamikaze pilot who is a protector as well as a driver. He is a jewel, being sure we don't pay too much for things. Learned a lot about bargaining from him. Stopped for a bucket of Kentucky Fried Chicken last week on the way home. As I was leaving, chicken in hand, a guy was selling bouquets of orchids - beautiful flowers. I thought it would be nice to take home with the chicken. He wanted 3,000 Rupiah, which is about $4. I offered him 1,000 Rp and finally paid him 2000 Rp ($3). Wish everything was as cheap. A jar of peanut butter costs about $6, and I do love peanut butter.

Friends of ours had an accident just before Christmas, and it sounded a bit familiar. Kirsten and her son Bryan, age 14, were in a crash on their way home. Bryan had a concussion & was out like a light at times, back on at others. His mom was bruised a bit, and he had his arm badly injured. They finally got to a hospital and had to wait two hours for the doctor to come. When he got there, he said it was too serious & they should take him to another hospital. They did and had to wait there for the doctor to arrive. Finally, 5 hours after the accident, he was treated by a doctor. He was in the hospital for three days, then ten days later, they decided his arm was broken and put him in a cast.

He is fine now. He spent a riotous weekend with your grandson on New Years, and they got along well. But as I consider the health care here, I get the willies. You can understand why companies send their people to Singapore for medical. That is how we justify a Singapore trip at Christmas time; the company pays for two medicals each year, one during home leave and the other at Christmas. We all got a clean bill of health this time. The Dr. (an Australian) says I've got the heart of a 30-year-old and all I have to do is lose 30 pounds. What does he know?

I've really been lucky here in Asia, haven't had any problem here in Jakarta, and that is something with all the critters in the air and water. I had one bout with the Asian quickstep when I was working in Malaysia while we were still in Singapore. I was working in Penang, getting to Singapore on the weekends, and got something in my system that almost did me in. I was working each day, then back to the rat trap where I was staying, where I'd sweat, chill, convulse, agonize, thought I was going to die, then wish I could. But after a few days, I outran it. Like they say here in Indonesia, Tidak Apa Apa, which literally means, "No, what what," but is used to express, "It doesn't matter." What does matter is all our love sent on this sunny day. Bob

The Indonesian language is interesting and not a difficult language to learn as languages go. As I learned more about it, I realized how very difficult English is and illogical. For instance, how would you pronounce 'OUGH?' Then think how tough it would be trying to learn English to be given the following words, Rough, Through, Plough, Although – you can probably think of a few others. Even those who speak pretty good English have a tough time with some of the sounds. TH in 'the' is not a sound they normally use; it usually sounds like a D. They do not have a sound equivalent to our 'U' as in up. They would say, 'oop.'

Fun-Ditty #3.1

"Any idiot can face a crisis... it's this day-to-day living that wears you out."

– Anton Chekhov.

3.2 – Freedoms

In Singapore, we had depended on our driver, provided by the company, for all our weekday needs. We had a similar arrangement in Jakarta those three years, but the car sat in the driveway for a few weekends before I decided to get a driver's license. This turned out to be an exciting experience.

There was one building in Jakarta (think of its size, about like Los Angeles, population over 7 million) to get a license (it's only a written test if you have one from abroad). All government offices and buildings had many uniformed police or military individuals standing by, so you didn't pay much attention.

Well, I went to a desk, followed the arrows, and selected the English form to fill out. I retired to a chair and desk for that purpose, and as I was studying the first question, a big brown finger came down and pointed to one of the multiple choices.

I looked up, and Dudley Do-Right was in full uniform with a pistol strapped to his hip and not a whisper of a smile. So I marked the one to which he was pointing. And the finger moved down the page, question by question, as I marked those so indicated. Was I going to argue with him?

As I finished the test, he moved back to the wall where he stood at attention. I took my test to the desk (it was in English) and passed with flying colors. I don't know yet what that was all about, but I was deemed legal on the road!

Armed now with a vehicle (our driver didn't work weekends), on a Saturday afternoon, I decided to drive to the next town, Bogor, about an hour's drive south. I was told there was a gong factory where they make the large gongs that hang in the hotel lobbies or museums. We had talked about getting one for some time.

Since the driver was out, I just hit the road myself, Bogor being about 40 miles south, a one-hour drive. It is a beautiful city, some 800 feet above Jakarta, that's a mountain, so to speak, where Sukarno, Indonesia's first president, spent most of his time when the nation was founded (~1965). I was sure I could find the place, that someone would tell me where it was when I got there. So there I was, a big country rube in a strange city, speaking a strange tongue.

I decided the best way to find the place was to park the car and take a taxi. The taxi I took was a "Bacek" (bay-chek), a three-wheeled bicycle with one passenger seat and a peddler. I tried to explain where I wanted to go, with hand motions showing how I would hit the gong with a dinger, or whatever it is called. After a bit, he seemed to know what I wanted, so away we went, across town, up hills, down hills; I would get out and walk up the hills with him. I was one of his heaviest loads.

Finally, we came to a ravine where he pointed down through some trees to the dark outline of a building. So I crossed the ravine on a narrow walkway, after convincing him to wait for me, climbed through a fence and down the hill through the trees, finding myself at the back entrance to a golf course clubhouse.

So, back up the hill, through the fence, across the ravine, to my little friend, where I re-explained where I wanted to go. Only this time, I explained with pictures as I drew my version of a gong on a slip of paper in my pocket. His face lit up as he finally understood, so back across town, up & down the hills, this about two hours after I had parked the car, we rounded a bend, and there it was, Goodyear Tire Company! So much for my drawing of a gong.

After a few more inquiries, I found a guy who spoke enough English and knew where the gong factory was. He asked, "You want to buy a gong? How much do you want to spend?" He told me to have the Bacek driver take me back to my car, then drive back to him, and he would take care of me! When I got back to the car, it was nearly dark, and I didn't want to be taken care of, so I drove back to Jakarta. Another time!

As residents of Indonesia, there is an issue of critters, something new and different. You've heard all the cockroach stories. Well, they are indeed a cunning adversary. Occasionally, I had to race from the yard to see who got to the open door first. You can't leave a door open for a moment. Norman Rockwell painted four pictures called the Four Freedoms: Freedom from fear, Freedom of speech, Freedom from hunger, and Freedom of worship. I love those four pictures, but I recently thought of the freedoms in the U.S. we take for granted and how neat it would be if he had painted more in the same line, such as:

> Freedom from cockroaches,
> Freedom from leaks,
> Freedom from power outages,
> Freedom from water outages,
> Freedom from telephone disruptions,
> Freedom from sticky handshakes,
> Freedom from Diarrhea...
> (to mention a few).

We had a delightful time in Singapore with our second child when we got our physicals. She stayed five days and then returned to Jakarta for the rest of her stay. My son had grown 3 1/2 inches since his physical last Christmas, and I think two more since our return. Good thing I can still whip him, but not much longer. (*I'm kidding.*)

Back in Jakarta, it rained like cats and dogs. We were in the rainy season and had a severe drought all summer and fall. It is supposed to start raining about Sept/Oct, but we didn't get any until December.

The genuine concern in many provinces was that the rice crop wouldn't feed the populace. But rain it does, when it does. It rains for about three months, some each day. There was a lot of concern about the lava flows at the active volcanoes, that the rains would start mudslides and wipe out some villages. The volcanoes decimated many areas during the previous year and usually made big headlines in the states.

I sometimes thought, as I drove past the serene scenes of happy Indonesian life, me worrying about this project and that manager, that debt, and who is really civilized. I was reminded of all the things I wanted to remember about this place. Public transportation was terribly essential here since most people didn't drive cars or even have them (you wouldn't think that as you saw the number of vehicles on the road, you'd think everyone was in a car). But Jakarta is the size of L.A., without the benefit of traffic flow systems or traffic lights on many busy intersections. Other 'not too busy' intersections don't even have stop signs, so you pick your way along carefully.

If you were to describe driving here, it would have to be called "offensive," not only that you might be offended by it, but more importantly, you are continually on the offensive as you drive. You don't worry about anyone in the rear as you drive. Instead, the tool for your success is your front fender. If you can get that one inch ahead of those to your left or right, then you have the right away. And try, you do!

I was careful to avoid fender benders when possible because, as a general rule of thumb, when an Expat gets in an accident, it is his fault. The reasoning is simple, if I had stayed in America where I belong, the accident would not have happened. So there was that hazard in driving there. I didn't do much driving with the family, except to church once in a while when I gave the driver the day off, or when I drove to the video shop to get something to watch at home on our company-provided video player.

We saw more movies in two weeks than we saw in a year in the states. At the video shop, we could rent a movie for about $1.00. A guy delivered for about $2.50. So on a good weekend, we would watch eight or ten movies, enjoy popcorn, and really live it up. I think we saw every film in Indonesia twice. I was so desperate once I even got "Tarzan," not for the kids!

When we went to Singapore, we always bought one or two good movies to keep and enjoyed watching them over and over. We had a few Disney's, including Fiddler on the Roof, which was always good. Electric Horseman that I watched and drooled over that Utah mountain country, Butch Cassidy and the Sundance Kid, and a couple of others. One we loved was "The Gods Must Be Crazy," the funniest show I had ever seen.

The family went to Singapore four days ahead of me to get the medicals taken care of, and on Wednesday evening, the night before I left, I attended the annual Christian Christmas program at the plant. It was an exciting mixture of traditional Javanese festivities and more modern Christian ceremonies. It showed with skits and pantomimes how the ancient religions there on the island of Java were replaced through the years with Christian tradition.

And they SANG! They sang with more gusto and enthusiasm than I have seen anyplace. It showcased a beautiful women's choir, and then at the end, three guys and a girl with a guitar sang, "I'll Be Home for Christmas," and it about did me in. It was the most beautiful song I had ever heard. It was only a few months later when our number two daughter (Lori) graduated from the Jakarta International School and did get to return to the homeland when she left for college.

Fun-Ditty #3.2

> "It is not the strongest of the species that survive, nor the most intelligent, but the one most responsive to change."
>
> *- Charles Darwin*
> *(1809-1882), British Scientist*

3.3 – The Affect

As we began our attempt to improve production at the Fairchild plant in Jakarta, we were faced with a monumental communication gap. Several leaders in the plant spoke good English, but very few second-level workers did. These were the important hands-on personnel who did the work.

My previous experience as a trainer/educator made me aware of the value of the personal connection, teacher-to-student. I wanted to capture that inner, feel-good domain called the Affect, which is the *emotional* dimension of a process, not typically considered in industry, and not considered deeply enough in other areas of life. Related to this concept is a quote I treasure, which reads, "I've learned that people will forget what you said, people will forget what you did, but people will never forget how you made them feel" - Maya Angelou.

I had learned about The Affect while conducting demonstrations in Milwaukee, like the ball floating in the flow with my classes. At that time there had been a growing interest in the world's literature about the domains of learning: Cognitive, Psychomotor, and Affective. What jumped out at me was the attention to the term "affective," which refers to results influenced by emotions.

Notice the ways these different domains are distinct from each other:

a) Cognitive - recognition in the *brain* and its role in solving mental tasks.
b) Psychomotor - *physical*, eye/hand coordination tasks.
c) Affective - how the student *feels* about the learning activity.

INDONESIA

I related well to the first two, but needed to learn how the "Affect" worked, or why it was important. While 'practicing' with my adult instrumentation students, I realized that the Affective domain was powerful, critical, and the least understood.

Folks in the sciences and math seemed to avoid the Affective domain since their areas are *not* emotional. What a waste! Play around with a fan/ball setup illustrated previously and see how *moving* the experience can be! The students love it and come back for more.

Giving proper, guided attention to *emotion* is a key to success. Yes, the Affect is yet another one of many secrets.

Tools for Generating Positive Emotions in the Workforce

1) Illusions in Marketing

Here is a feel-good 'aha' to which workers will relate. Ask them which gray square is larger, the left one, or the right? The point, of course, is they are the same size. But the surrounding lines make the left one stand out, seeming larger. So what's the message? Pay attention to what's important, and don't be distracted by large fluff. We often miss the most important things when we give attention to distractions in the peripheral.

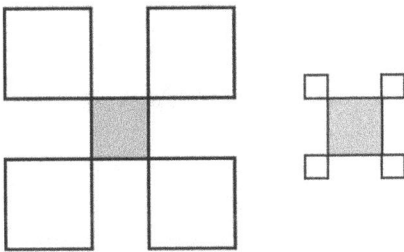

For example, think of a product as an object surrounded by a cluster of advertising, marketing, and sales promotions, like the squares surrounding the gray figure in the center above. When these promotions and programs are understated (smaller), the quality of the product (the inner square) appears greater. If the advertising, marketing, and sales promotions are over the top, the quality of the product itself appears less than it really is. This principle can help us "under promise and over deliver," aiding in the company's or product's positive reputation and customer satisfaction. This visual can be a powerful tool for helping those who determine the advertising dollars for the product make wise decisions

2) Thinking Out of the Box

I gave my workers (students) the following dots on a plain piece of paper:

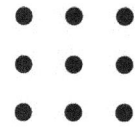

Then I asked them to connect these nine dots with four straight lines without lifting the pencil from the paper: Here's what they will try.

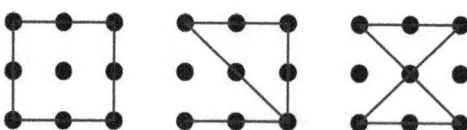

Next, I showed them the simple solution.

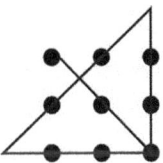

The first time I showed this to my grandkids, they said, "That's cheating!" They were taught to draw within the lines. We must break the mindset that all lines must stay within the box. This is where the metaphor started, "Think outside the box!"

In my experience, this little activity connects with students of all ages. And they feel good about it.

But what's the value here? It's up to us to examine every aspect of our workday, workplace, and work mindset to find the little things to make it all work better (smarter). Each time we consider that word "better," substitute "smarter" to help get that added 30% from the team. It's up to us! And it's up to "them."

I then asked them to connect the nine dots with only THREE straight lines without lifting the pencil from the paper!

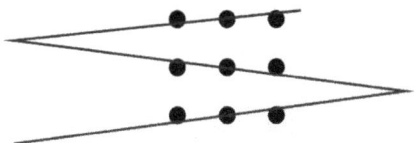

Lastly, I challenged them to connect all dots with a single line. (How about with a paintbrush?)

3) Remembering the Affect

Thinking outside the box doesn't always mean finding better ways to accomplish a task. Sometimes it means being more attuned to the Affect, or the emotional aspect of an experience for those involved. For example, managers at a local bank tried to speed up the traffic flow, reducing time-to-wait for those standing in line. They found many customers hated the hurry-hurry, rather enjoying the time to visit other like-minded clients. We must ask ourselves: how important is it to understand all aspects of each situation before applying smart solutions?

It was a rewarding experience, learning how to bring the Affect into my management role with my trainees in Jakarta. But ultimately, my three-year contract in Indonesia ended and we were soon enough on our way back to the States. However, this was not my last jaunt as an expat. New challenges taking me to another corner of the world where I would uncover even more secrets, were already on the horizon.

Fun-Ditty #3.3

> *"Education is not the filling of a pail, but the lighting of a fire."*
>
> *- William Butler Yeats*

NOTES FOR CHAPTER 3

Additional thoughts related to this chapter:

Count the Fs

Here's another fun exercise that can be conducted with management teams, friends, or grandchildren, as long as they speak English. It works best if you issue the challenge verbally:

Count the Fs in the following sentence:

> Finished files are the result of years of scientific study and years of practice. Did you count three? There are six Fs; however, the F in "of" sounds like a "V," it seems to disappear, and most adults will count only three. What's the lesson here?

Foundry

A foundry producing 350 tons of gray iron castings per month had a high rejection rate of 21%. An equally high percentage (20%) of castings (20%) were also rejected during machining. An early survey revealed that the operational managers weren't aware of quality, technological improvements were slow, and manufacturing systems and procedures were not well-defined.

Thus, the operational managers received training in quality management and problem-solving tools, their commitment to the quality improvement program was obtained, and they initiated quality improvement projects at the management level. These steps helped bring down the rejection rate to around 14% in a year, but it remained stagnant at that rate during the next six months.

At this point, management decided to involve workers in quality improvement activities. A cross-level team consisting of the general manager, departmental heads, shop supervisors, inspectors, and shop-floor workers was formed. The team reviewed the foundry scrap on the shop floor daily at a set time and place. In these meetings, rejects were discussed, their causes were identified, corrective actions were planned, and responsibility for the corrective actions was assigned to various team members.

The rejection rate dropped to less than 6% in one month. Other benefits were also realized:

1. Top management's support of and involvement in quality improvement activities became evident.
2. Employees at all levels became concerned about quality.
3. The pace of identifying the root causes of problems and developing corrective actions was accelerated.
4. Employees' morale was boosted
5. They gained confidence in their ability to perform better.

What conclusions can you draw from this case study about the difference between the early approach and that taken later? What is the most important single point that contributed to the later success? Could this approach be used in a non-manufacturing enterprise, such as a hospital?

Additional details from the letter to my mother

I also said:

> *Funny thing, last month before Christmas, one of the Indonesians in our office quit, and we gave him a farewell dinner at a place called the Green Pub, which specialized in Mexican food, of all things. Pretty good. And they have a live country & western band, all Indonesians. You couldn't tell the difference between a good old honky tonk in the states except for a few sounds. We had them play as a request 'Take this job and shove it!' They did it perfectly except for the word shove, which came out with a long O,*

as in stove. One of our friends, the Matellis, was having a birthday dinner for one of their daughters, and Ray stopped at our table in the midst of 'San Antonio Rose' to say how good it was to hear some Christmas music at this time. They were from somewhere in Texas.

Bali Trip

This narrative describes our family trip from Jakarta across the island of Java to the island of Bali. It did not include our eldest daughter, who had recently begun university studies. Lori had also left the nest but flew in from the states for our trip. I wrote the following in my journal:

Day 1 – Well, here we are on the way to Bali this Sunday afternoon. Lori came by surprise yesterday. That is, we didn't expect her until late today. But the itinerary was written wrong by the travel agent, so she took a cab home from the airport, arriving at about 8 am. I traveled to Singapore yesterday for a job interview with a company in Bangkok. The job has possibilities.

Anyway, I returned from Singapore last night, getting to the airport about one hour after Lori. Lili, our driver, waiting for me, saw her and said to himself, that's her! But no, Mrs. Robertson said not 'til tomorrow. So she walked right past him, and he didn't say anything. She surprised me, being home already when I arrived.

Back to the story! We went to church today. Lori slept in, having spent the last two days in airplanes and a night layover in Tokyo. We got home at about 11:30 & packed up to make our getaway for the week. Dan and Leslie have the week off for the Easter break, and we've planned for two years to drive to Bali to see the sights. We have been in Indonesia for nearly three years and haven't seen

Bali, a shameful state of affairs! So when Lori decided to come for a rest, we asked if she could come early enough to make the trip with us. She took some tests early, so we are now together in the VW bus, with Lili driving us to our first stop, Bandung, the first leg of a long trip. It's about a 24-hour journey in total. We plan on spending two nights in Yogyakarta. Then on to Bali for three nights.

My youngest (Leslie) who was about 12 had an opportunity to go to Bali with the senior class for Jakarta International School, as one of her friends' folks is a senior class sponsor going to Bali with the seniors for their senior trip. She was able to fill in for a senior who couldn't make it. So she left Saturday with the group, and we will meet her in Bali to return together. She hasn't seen her older sister yet.

We are now in the bus trucking over Puncak pass on our way to Bandung. Finally left the house at about 3 pm. Just ahead of us on this climb over the pass is a large passenger bus that reminds us of 'The Gods must be Crazy' because there is one guy at the back door hanging out with a large rock on the step. He jumps out each time the traffic stalls and puts the rock behind the wheel to keep it from crashing back down the hill onto us.

We arrived in Bandung at about 7:30 and stayed at Panghegar, a nice hotel with all the services. A very good day.

Day 2 – We left Bandung after a good evening's rest at about 7:30. After driving for 8 hours, we arrived in Yogyakarta at 4:30 pm. President Jones of the mission presidency had given the name of the Branch Pres. in Yogya. We had ordered batik murals of church history scenes from Sis. Moerjito in Jakarta last year. Her husband knew an artisan in Yogja who did this, and he showed us samples we were impressed with. Before we received the batiks, Bro Moerjjto died, and his wife left for Yogya, and we lost track of her.

We had more or less dropped the idea. But when planning this trip, we thought we would talk to the Branch Pres. in Yogya to see if we could find Sis. Moerjito. So that led us to Pres. Jones for the address for the Branch Pres. in Yogya, Hadi Pranoto. So, after checking into the hotel, we got back in the car with Lili, leaving my middle two at the hotel, and set out to find the address. After about an hour of driving and asking questions of many pedestrians and bystanders (Indonesian note: it seems to be contrary to the culture ever to say they "don't know." So much of the guidance received in an address search as this is questionable). We arrived at a dark alleyway, into which Lili disappeared for what seemed like 30 minutes, returning with an Indonesian gentleman who turned out to be the branch president, Pres. Pronoto.

He got into the car with us as it was raining and discussed through Lili (Pres. Pronoto did not speak any English) the escapade with the Moerdjitos and the batik paintings. He told us Sister Moerjito had long since returned to Jakarta, and Bro Simpson had taken the batik paintings to the states. So there we were. We asked if we could possibly meet the artist and perhaps order more? It was difficult communicating as he just kept saying, through Lili, that there was no more stock.

He invited us into his house, down the dark alley, where we found out that he was indeed the artist and that he had pictures of the church scenes we wanted and could, in *fact, order them right there. A young man was in his home named Johnny, who had served a mission a couple of years ago in the Indonesian Mission and spoke English. We worked through him and ordered six scenes. It will take two months to finish the lot, and he only wanted $12.00 each. These are real works of art, handcrafted, taking two months to complete, for which there will never be another, just like the ones made for us.*

We bought two small batik's he had finished and left a deposit for the others. We will correspond by mail to get them paid for and delivered. It was a very interesting experience. And Lili had a very good experience with Indonesian Mormons as he discussed tomorrow's trip to the Borobudur temple with other family members in an adjoining room. Another very good day.

Day 3 & 4 – We started this day with Lili picking up Johnny, the young man living with Pak Pranoto, who stayed home from his university studies to guide us to the sights this day. They picked us up at the hotel at 8 am, and we traveled first to the Borobudur temple. This magnificent edifice has been restored over the past several years. It is a very large shrine built on levels depicting the Buddhist belief that there are three levels or degrees in life. The temple has ten levels or steps, which somehow designate the three levels of life. It is difficult to describe just how magnificent the whole thing really is. Hopefully, our pictures will do it some justice.

After a couple of hours, we returned for a quick look at the sultan's palace but decided not to go in. We next went to an address Lili had, the only Bonsai garden in Indonesia. The owner was an ex-soldier in Sukarno's army, and in 1945 he studied under the Chinese and learned the ancient art of Banzai. His Banzai has been honored and taken to Suharto's palace and has successfully grown a Bonsai coconut tree that is four feet high and about forty years old and had grown one coconut. He says it takes over twenty years to grow one coconut.

We saw giant Banyan trees in Sumatra last December, with massive root systems growing into the ground. The trunks were probably 20 feet across. The roots, very strangely, would come down from the massive limbs and then grow into the ground, forming small room-like passages. This Banzai artist in Yogya has grown a Bonsai Banyan tree about three feet high. Lili seemed disappointed we wouldn't buy one to take home with us. He would like one himself, but their cost was between $200 and $500 each.

After a quick stop at a silversmith to get a look at Yogya silverwork, we made another quick stop at Kentucky Fried Chicken, then Lili dropped us off at the hotel and took Johnny home. We checked out at 1 pm and decided to get a jump on the long ride to Bali. Figured we could go as far as Mudian and spend the night there. That would be about a four-hour drive, which would then reduce the final leg of the trip to Bali to about eight hours. If we stayed the night in Yogya as we had originally planned, it would be a 12 to 14-hour drive. So, we left the hotel, packed up, and filled with the Colonel's Fried Chicken at 1:15 pm. We stopped for about 20 minutes at the Candi Prambanan, only 2 KM from the hotel (Candi is the word for temple, pronounced "Channdy," which is a Hindu temple of the same vintage as the Borobudur (the Borobudur temple is Buddhist)… and on we went.

After discussing the matter with Lili, we decided to drive straight through, all the way to Bali. That would save a hotel bill that night, and as the kids would be sleeping most of the way, the long trip would not be the same problem. We felt like Lili needed some rest before beginning the long night on the road. So we decided a movie would be in order in the early evening if we could find one, and Lili could then rest. Well, we did find a theater in a relatively small city, which had started 30 minutes earlier, and they wouldn't seat you after the flick had started.

So, back into the car and on to the next town to try again. Success! We found one that was ready to start in about 15 minutes. So wait, we did. Certainly, the fairest-skinned troop seen around that location in many a year. Everyone seemed to get quite a kick out of us waiting, also. So in we went and sat in the middle section. All seats around us quickly filled up with Indonesians, who, five minutes after the flick had started, seemingly on cue, lit up their Indonesian clove cigarettes. My wife and Lori decided to go to the lobby, wait a few minutes, then find another seat in some remote location. My son and I followed a few minutes later, but in the lobby, we decided that wasn't for us, so we returned to the car and were on our way. Lili, all the time, was agreeable and understanding. He told me, 'Indonesian people always do that, where it says 'Don't smoke,' they smoke. Where it says 'Don't park,' they park.'

So, through the night, we drove. I sat in front talking with Lili, my wife in the far back with Lori asleep on her lap, and our son asleep across the near back seat. Lili told me about the wildlife living in that part of Java. He said if we watched closely, we might see the black panther

INDONESIA

(or leopard, I'm not sure) that is plentiful. It is against the law to shoot this animal in Indonesia. We didn't see one crossing the road, but Lili came bolting back into the car at one point, seeing one in the bushes where he was relieving himself.

We arrived at the car ferry to take us to the island of Bali from the far east end of Java at 3:30 am. After a 40-minute ferry ride, we were finally on the island of Bali. It was another two hours to the city of Danpasar where our hotel was. We were able to check into our rooms at 8 am, where we cleaned up and took a two-hour snooze. We got our act together just after 2 pm and called our youngest, who had been there since Saturday with the senior class. Our middle two went down to the beach and snorkeled. The air-con in the rooms was the pits, so we checked out the hotel where our reservations had us the next two days, finding it close and less expensive. We considered checking out, but it would cost us 50% of the fare where we first checked in. This Nusa Dua Beach Hotel is quite new and very nice and expensive, but clear out in the boonies on the southern tip of the island, about a half-hour by car to the next anything.

We drove just after dark to see Leslie where she was staying at the Kartika Plaza Hotel and stopped at the familiar house of the Colonel on the way for some finger-licking chicken. After we had finished our meal, which was served on large porcelain plates, I stood up and walked to the large metal garbage can and just tipped the tray, so all the goodies dropped into the can the way I have done it a hundred times. I forgot that the large plate was not disposable, which made a terrific crash as it hit the bottom of the large metal can. Everyone in the place turned their stare on stupid Me. Talk about embarrassing. And m'own family laughed loudest!

We did find her, who had been in an accident where a motorcycle hit her bicycle the day before. She was unconscious for only about five minutes. Scarfed up her knee a bit. After a visit and planning session, we returned to our hotel. The seniors are leaving tomorrow morning, so Lili will pick her up and bring her to our hotel first. Our son and I went down and saw a movie in the hotel video room (no TVs in the room). Then back to the typewriter for this two-day summary account. These have not been the best two days of my life. Hopefully, tomorrow will bring great and exciting developments.

Day 5 - We checked out of the hotel at about 7 am, then waited in the lobby for her, who arrived with Lili at about 7:40 am. I had misunderstood the desk clerk about making plans for a tour this day. It seems I should have made reservations yesterday; oops!

So we went to the other hotel, not too far away. Lori and I walked over. It wasn't as elaborate as the first, but adequate. Lili brought the other bags, then. Hardly knew what to do with the day. Lili took my son and me to the Kuta Beach area to check out renting motorcycles driving about 20 minutes away. Found a rental, but my Indonesian license was grade "A," My son didn't have one, and Lili's was grade "C," as required. After some persuasion, he rented us two bikes, one road bike, and one trailer bike, on Lili's license. It cost us about $32.00 for both, for two days. The guy asked me if I'd ever driven one before. I said sure, once. That was in Moab on Ken Stile's bike in 1972. I think it was around the block once. I got on, Lili showed me how to get it started & away we went, charging down a small, busy Indonesian-type street. It killed on me after about a half-block & I couldn't get it started again.

So Lili finally came running down & suggested I drive the bus and follow him and our son on the bikes until we got out of town, where he would give me some quick instructions. So I did, and we did, and he did, and we trucked back to the hotel like Marlin Brando or Peter Fonda at about 11:00. Lori was asleep on the couch in the lobby; she transferred to the hotel room to resume her sleep. Dan, Leslie and I went to the recreation room, where we watched a video, "H-Bomb," a spy thriller. Leslie slept with her head in my lap while I dozed on and off through the movie. I think our son saw it all.

My wife took Lili on a short tour while we watched the flick & saw some neat stuff we must see tomorrow. After the video, we got on the bikes and cruised around the hotel. I initially took Leslie back with me for a while, but she is not in love with motorcycles, so she didn't stay very long. So our son and I snooped around in the boonies near the hotel. At about 4:30, we all gathered and went to Kuta Beach to swim and try the surf. Leslie and I were the only ones to get into the water, but it was great. The biggest surf I've ever experienced. When we would jump to catch a big wave to body surf, it would just throw me every way but loose, and each time I would come up with my swimming suit around my ankles. Kind of a new look on the beach!

But it was nearly dark, so we only stayed for a short time. After a bit of shopping in the stalls by the beach, we stopped at a good booth and ordered two bags full of fried *bananas. We then trucked back to the hotel, where we all crapped out. A better day!*

Day 6 - My wife woke with a bang, with a noise that we should get on the trail since it is the last day before we leave. Our flight was scheduled for 9:00 am on Saturday, and here it was Friday. So while we got ourselves ready, she took the horse carriage down to the beach where she met a boy named Rachman who was going to Surabaya Saturday on his motorcycle!

We met the tour guide at the hotel lobby at 8 am, who we had booked the day before, then waited for my wife, who missed the return horse carriage from the beach and had to walk. Here she came, with tell-tale sand and moisture on the bottom of her Levi's. I didn't ask any questions, and away we went for a day of Bali tour.

The guide was a happy little guy with reams of info on Bali in his mind that just kept pouring off his tongue. And when he realized after about 30 minutes that nobody was listening to him, he just turned around and kept on talking to himself. Our first stop was the Monkey Forest, where hundreds of monkeys were in a gorgeous forest of very tall trees. They are camp robbers of the worst breed and expect you to feed them after entering the forest. And they are all over you.

One of the guys held a banana over my wife's head until one jumped on her head. Then he said, holding his polaroid camera in his hand, 'Do you want a picture?' He wanted $2.00, but she would only offer him 50 cents, so he went away. But the monkey wouldn't get off. But then, as I walked on the scene, one of the blasted things jumped on my shoulder and proceeded to relieve himself, totally *without even saying thanks! I got him off at once, and our guide cleaned it off with leaves as best he could. But I shortly went into a stall, bought myself a Bali shirt, and walked out with a newspaper-wrapped package under my arm.*

Then on to the volcano and a view of Gunung Agung, the biggest volcano on the island. A fantastic sight with an enormous crater, probably over 10 miles across, with a large lake and the cone of the latest volcano rising high from the center of the crater. This volcano erupted in 1969, and you can see the lava flow paths down its side and into the lake.

We had lunch at a restaurant just before the volcano. Our guide expressed sincere interest in our church as we traveled and asked many good questions at the restaurant. He is protestant but a native of Bali with much history and traditional ties to the local Hindu religion. You see, Indonesia was once Hindu, and when the Muslim faith moved in a few hundred years ago, the Hindu people moved to East Java and finally found their home on the island of Bali. It is not the same exacting Hindu religion found in India, but a blend seemingly of Balinese culture and Hinduism. Cows are eaten in Bali. Their main meat is pork and beef.

After the volcano and many pictures, we started back towards Denpasar and stopped by a turtle farm (so-called) which is a staging area for turtles imported from other islands and then picked up by trucks or cars to be taken to restaurants & markets around the island. Turtle meat is forbidden to Muslims, but no problem in Bali with the Hindus. They eat 80 tons of turtles in Bali each year.

By now, it is around 4 pm, and little time to get to the Cliff Shrine my wife saw with Lili yesterday, so we asked if he could drive fast. Whew!! We dropped our guide off at the hotel. Then on to a shrine built on a very high cliff overlooking the ocean on the island's southern tip. It had dozens of monkeys, of which I stayed clear, and a breathtaking scene of the sunset into the ocean in the west (yes, it still sets in the west in this part of the world).

Back to the hotel with dinner on our mind, Leslie had trouble finding something on the menu that she liked, so we planned on our son and Lili driving back to Kuta Beach and KFC on the motorcycles. We are now waiting for their return, having eaten supper from the hotel menu without them. I hope they return. They returned unscathed—an evening on the motorcycles without a scratch.

Day 7 - This day began as I left the room at about 6:30 with everyone else asleep. I had Lili drive me to the American Express office above Denpasar, about an hour's drive, to see if I could get some cash to tide us over. You see, our plane tickets had us all leaving at 9:30 this morning for the return to Jakarta, with Lili driving back across Java by himself. We got the tickets changed until Sunday at 3 pm, and my wife and Lori decided to drive back with Lili since they didn't have to be back to Jakarta for any pressing reasons, such as work or school. So we need a bit of Uang ($), as they say in Indonesia.

The Amex office had to telex Jakarta for approval, so I had to be back about 11:30 to pick up the Uang if approved. I stopped at Galael's, the western-type grocery store, picked up some peanut butter, jam, and bread, all the essentials for any trip or occasion, and returned to the hotel at 9:30 am. My wife stayed at the hotel and got into the culture and ways of life with a book on Bali.

Lili & I took the kids to Kuta beach, where we dropped them off for a couple of hours on the good Indonesian surf. After Lili and I finished our business with Amex, we started back to get the kids when a motorcycle ran into our side and messed the driver up a bit. Lili jumped out, assessed the situation, ran back to the car, got his first-aid kit out, went back & pushed the bike off the road, bandaged up the driver, and they were arm in arm by the time we left. The guy even apologized for running into us. Lili is an exceptional person. I wish we could take him with us wherever we go.

Here's a note on yesterday's visit to the volcano as an insight into the routine you follow when you go to the trinket or clothing stalls where the hawkers ply their trade. One of the little gals was trying to sell Lori something at one stall, and the conversation went something like this: 'You want to buy this? Only 4,000 rupiahs.' Ours said no, but the vendor came back in muffled tones, kind of under her breath, 'You don't say no, you say maybe 2,000 rupiahs, then I say maybe okay, 3,000 rupiahs,' with kind of a giggle. Lori got quite a kick out of that kind of that approach.

"After getting the kids back to the hotel, my wife and I went with Lili to look for genuine sandalwood fans, something she had read about in one of the books. One magazine suggested one good place to buy with a price that indicated that it looked much better than anything she had seen before. So with the scant instructions in the magazines given to Lili, away we went. It only took him six question stops to find the place. Still open though it was now after

dark, it was the genuine true scented sandalwood fans at the place where they are manufactured with the owner & main artisan present. The price was about double what the article suggested, which got the owner a bit uptight. He was ready to call the guy who did the photographs for the article, who he knows well, and find out where he got such info! A very interesting side trip.

"We returned to the hotel to find the kids in the rec room watching a video, and the evening came to an end. A good day.

"Day 8 - We boarded our flight the next morning, taking us back to our home in Jakarta. Lili began the long drive back. A very good experience."

Letter Home

Following is a letter I wrote to my mom, a widow living in the small town where she'd been born.

22 March 1982 – Jakarta, Indonesia

Dear Mom, Just sitting here in this big empty house all alone, so better drop you a line. The family is all at play practice. I was scheduled to go to Singapore today at 6 pm on business but found out at the last minute they hadn't renewed my exit visa. Very touchy about that. You have to get government permission to leave or enter. Of course, there is always a fee for the privilege.

Anyway, I left the house this morning with my suitcase and said my goodbye's to everyone. Then I was going to the airport from work. But had to come home, finding the whole family at play practice until late tonight. The play opens this week Wednesday, running four nights until Saturday. It is going to be so good; I'd give anything if you could see it. I'm sure you've heard much about the trauma of her not getting the lead role, but life goes on.

We have been planning our home leave for the last few weeks, looking at going through Europe and New York that way, then going through Australia and the South Pacific Islands and on to Los Angeles. And stars in the eyes and high hopes. But when you get right down to it, there is a little more involved. The company only provides round-trip airfare to our home from Jakarta, with four weeks to do it. When hotel rooms, meals, cars, laundry, and all else that goes with travel are considered, it loses its appeal. The reason we are in Asia is to pay our bills and get out of debt and pay for the two beautiful young ladies to go to the university, and not too far away, a mission for a third (number one grandson) kinder along with school, and on and on.

Anyway, what is a possibility at this point is going to Australia (the company requires that we get out of town), flying our oldest out to meet us there, and then the two girls can fly back to the states together to attend school. Only a thought at this point. If we did that, it would mean over $5,000 in our pocket since the company would give us the cash for the round-trip fare to Salt Lake City. We would retire two delinquent debts in Orem with that.

Having some excitement over here now. This is an election year, and the elections are in May. There are three parties in the system, one in power is called Golkar, which is the most progressive, accepting foreigners and business influences from outside. Another is a radical Muslim party, like Khomeini's group in Iran, and a third is quite left-leaning. Anyway, the campaigning got underway last week at a rally with many thousands of participants. Ended up in a riot with many injured and stores and businesses ransacked. The embassy closed down and told all expats to stay home. It wasn't as bad as it sounded, more like a high-school rumble, but with the numbers of people involved, it could get out of hand.

Work is so busy I'm really pooped out. Looking forward to Easter weekend as we will take a few days and do something; not sure just what yet. We'll send you pictures of whatever it is.

Really a nice homecoming tonight, two letters from our oldest and the two (in one envelope) from you. Keep up the good work.

P.S. Your birthday gift is on a slow boat from China… Much love, Bob."

CHAPTER 4

Arizona, New York, Ohio

4.0 – Standing for Quality

After three years in Indonesia, Intel recruited me as a Training Manager at a new startup factory in Arizona. Most companies that make Integrated Circuits (ICs) operate in off-shore locations to take advantage of low labor costs. However, Intel chose to buck that trend and find profit stateside. While at Intel, I increased my understanding of quality principles and began to sell my services, teaching quality principles in Arizona at Motorola. Our son Dan finished high school while we lived there and began his engineering studies at a university twelve hours north.

Malcolm Baldrige was Secretary of Commerce under President Ronald Reagan, playing a major role in influencing Administration trade policy and taking the lead in resolving difficulties with China and India. Baldrige held the first Cabinet-level talks with the Soviet Union, paving the way for increased access for U.S. firms. The Malcolm Baldrige National Quality Award was created in his honor.

My Motorola experience connected me with different people in the business at a time when quality was in huge demand. It was the Malcolm Baldrige National Quality award that took us to New York in 1988 where I would spend three years as Quality Manager at Standard Microsystems Corporation (SMC) on Long Island.

Design of Experiments (DOE)

While I was at Motorola, I learned about Experimental Design, which is any industrial process that is made up of many factors acting together. For example, in a foundry, variables might include the percentage of clay in the sand, compressibility of the sand mix, the temperature of the iron as it is poured into the sand mold, the time the casting stays in the mold, and many other factors relating to iron chemistries.

I learned that it would be in the company's interest to ask: How do we find the combination of all these factors together to obtain the best result? What is the best recipe?

The same questions can be asked of the recovery process in gold mill operations; time/temp relationships in the roaster, time/pressure/temp relationships in the autoclave, chemical recovery from gold-loaded carbon, etc. Each process has multiple variables that impact process performance. So, one would wonder: What would a 5% improvement in yield be worth to a company over a year in one of these processes? Or a 15% reduction in the cost of a reclamation process?

It had been a long-standing tradition (a classical method) to address this question by holding all factors constant except one, then adjust that one to find the best level. Next, repeat for the next factor, the next, and the next. This was essentially the Scientific Model that students typically learn in high school.

However, this approach requires (assumes) *uniform conditions* for all factors except the one being observed. This approach is unwanted for two reasons:

1. *Uniform conditions* are a myth. They never exist. Imposing artificial conditions creates a process environment quite different from reality. The results cannot be repeated in the field.
2. It is usually not advisable to try to hold all factors constant except one because there are often interaction effects between factors that are more important than any direct effect. This occurs whenever the effect produced by one factor is modified by changes in the other.

Therefore, a well-designed experiment (aka DOE) is a series of trials planned by smart people (note the plural), including *all* relevant factors (variables), sufficient in number to screen out system variation and noise, arranged in a pattern to provide maximum information. Whew! (Note we are not just looking for *data*, but for all *information* that may have a bearing on our results).

Since U.S. companies face stiff competition in the global market, DOE is a strategic weapon to fight this technical battle. Many feel DOE is too costly and should remain in the laboratories. However, a simple DOE is the most cost-effective way to gather this information. For instance, a staggering five factors (variables) can be studied in one 16-run fractional factorial experiment without disturbing the process. It provides information on all five factors, as well as the ten two-factor interactions present.

Obtaining this much information would otherwise require 80 runs to get the same precision from a one-at-a-time experiment with no measure of interactions!

The lesson in this is reminiscent of the lessons we learned about Variation, to trust that optimal results can be obtained if we take a less rigid approach in both data analysis, and in life.

Fun-Ditty #4.0

> *"If you think education is expensive – try ignorance."*
> *- Derek Bok*

4.1 — Why Quality?

Armed with powerful tools to improve quality, then what can (should) we do with them? Massive and continual training!!! Learning is vital. But equally important is the retention of lessons learned. We must focus on methods and processes. The lessons we learn must be woven into the fabric of the organization, and where the principles are universal, also into our lives.

There IS a best-known way (not necessarily the best way) to do *anything*, and we must discover what that is and then *improve* it. But the key is to retain, to store those lessons learned into the "memory" of the company. Otherwise, we all go up our learning curves inefficiently, reinventing the wheel with each new project.

If anyone finds a better way, we must capture that learning. We can learn a great deal from others. Americans have been recognized as leaders in innovation, but not in every case. The Germans invented the gasoline-powered car, but it took Henry Ford to give customers a cheap reliable vehicle. The Germans were also the first to use jet airplanes, but it was the Americans who eventually capitalized on the commercial possibilities of jet aviation.

The British invented most of the tools of mass production, but the Americans applied them to commercial use. The culture of our organization must support these efforts to learn and improve. Paramount in this learning and training effort is the understanding of the intimate connection between the rate of learning and the rate of improvement. In no better place is this true than in the everyday use of statistics in the learning process, stimulating how we think about learning. Statistics provide a common language of improvement.

If we consider training as simply the cost of doing business rather than an investment with an expected return, that is what we'll get. How training is to be staged is an important output of a quality council. Expectations are wonderful.

Learning is the new form of labor. It is no longer a separate activity that occurs *before* one enters the workplace or in remote class settings. Learning is the *heart* of proactive activities. This moves us into a dynamic world instead of a static one, where continual change and improvement are the norms.

Training employees to the hilt and encouraging them to develop themselves at company expense is how organizations pay for the right to demand loyalty. It's also part of the price they pay for the privilege of operating in a free country.

> *I would soon discover what must be overcome in order to apply these principles in a country which*

has not always shared the same freedoms as we enjoy in the United States.

Still, during my tenure as a Quality instructor in New York, I used examples like the following to teach some of the most profound principles of Quality Control in my classes:

Excerpts from "I Believe I'll Have the Reuben" by Richard I. Ferrin

WHAT MAY I GET FOR YOU today, gentlemen?" asked the man behind the Nine-to-Five Deli counter in Maryville, TN. Little did I know that this question would lead to a gut-level understanding of total quality management, free from the usual jargon.

I studied the menu board above the man's head and spotted the words "Reuben sandwich." I love Reuben's, but only if the corned beef is lean, the sauerkraut plentiful and well-cooked, and the bread lightly toasted.

"Are your Reuben's good?" I asked. "The best," the man said. "Really?" I told him I used to work in New York City and have sampled some pretty good Reuben's. "Do you really believe your Reuben's are the best?" "You decide," he said.

Aha No. 1: The customer determines the quality of a product or service, not the maker or purveyor. The customer is free to use any standard they choose. It could be from the memory of the ideal Reuben frequently ordered for lunch at a tiny take-out deli on 57th Street, or the memory of the Reuben once shared with someone special at an outdoor grill alongside a harbor in Florida. It doesn't matter.

> *I studied the menu board for another minute and then said, "I believe I'll have the Reuben." My friend Bill, who also had been studying the board trying to decide from the five types of meat, six kinds of cheese, and four types of bread, said, "I believe I'll have a Reuben, too."*
>
> *We found a booth and waited. The man turned to his wife and announced our order. They set about making two of the best Reubens they could. Before long, he proudly set the creations before us....*
>
> *I remember commenting, "These are pretty good Reuben's, don't you think?" Bill agreed, and that was that.*

Aha No. 2: If you are the supplier of goods or services, you might think that your customers are focusing on the quality of what you have provided. You have knocked yourself out, and you want them to notice. But, horrors, they often don't unless the product is obviously awful or absolutely terrific. If it's just satisfactory or even pretty good, they might very well take it for granted.

> *When I had about two bites left in my Reuben, the man came out from behind the counter and*

> approached our booth. "Well," he asked, "how is the sandwich?"

Aha No. 3: The only way to get an accurate understanding of your product is to ask the customer. Standing in the kitchen in a spasm of self-congratulation for outdoing yourself won't tell you what you need to know. Your best judgment is no substitute for getting direct feedback from the object of your intentions.

> *Being an educator, when I think of evaluation, my mind instinctively zooms to grades. Shame on me. "An A-," I said, grading his sandwich.*
>
> *"What do I have to do to get an A+?" was his quick response.*
>
> *I was ready with an answer. "It could use a little more sauerkraut." Frankly, to this day, I don't know whether or not the little deli on 57th Street piled on more sauerkraut than the deli in Maryville. It just seemed that the sandwich would be better and deserving of an A+ if it had more fermented cabbage.*

Aha No. 4: Most customers have an unspoken standard, even though they might never have tried to articulate it. Guessing what that standard is or becoming defensive about falling short of some unknown, fantasized ideal isn't likely to lead to improvement that fully satisfies customers. Never mind the wasted time and vain flailing. I couldn't believe what had happened next. Even though Bill and I were nearly finished, the man went back to the kitchen, pulled a fistful of cold sauerkraut from a container, and was about to plop it on the grill for a minute. Then I heard his wife say, "But that's all we have."

> *"But we can get an A+," the man said with total seriousness. And on the grill went the whole load."*

Aha No. 5: You have to really care about getting an A+. In just a few minutes, the man was back at our booth with a plateful of steaming sauerkraut. Watching the kitchen scene unfold, Bill and I stopped eating. It would have been a pity to have finished our sandwiches before he got back.

> *We stuffed as much sauerkraut as we could into our remaining sandwich portions, sprinkled them with mustard, and polished them off.*

Aha No. 6: If you really want an A+ and if you really are committed to total quality management, you had better not just meet customers' expectations but exceed them. If you meet their expectations, customers might be satisfied but are not necessarily going to rave about the experience.

> *Translated into higher-education terminology, a student whose expectations were met in the past academic year might regard the experience as having been a "good year." Still, other urges might persuade them to transfer to another school. If expectations are exceeded, the student is more inclined to feel that they are getting great value and a contagious level of commitment.*

> *I suspect the man at the deli didn't make much money on the Rueben's that Bill and I ordered that day, but he clearly established us as repeat customers. What's more, I've told this story to hundreds of people since that day, and some of them surely have found their way to the Nine-to-Five Deli in Maryville.*
>
> *Quality service pays, and it's not that complicated to provide.*
>
> *(FERRIN, Richard I. I believe I'll have the Reuben. Quality Progress. May, 1994.)*

Imagine what could happen if we applied these principles not just in industry, but also in our personal lives.

The Tortoise vs. The Hare

In my work, I discovered there are distinct differences in preferred managerial practices between America and Japan. These differences can be illustrated by the story of the tortoise and the hare, in which the slow, steady tortoise defeats the fast-starting hare in a race.

American managers (using the hare approach) prefer drastic changes in large leaps. Individual crusaders often lead these changes at the top management level. Japanese managers (using the tortoise approach) pursue incremental improvements within the framework of available organizational resources, existing structures, and core competencies. They involve teams of employees not necessarily from the top of the company hierarchy.

(This comparison between the top-down and bottom-up approaches has been polarized. In real life, successful corporate managers do not strictly use either of the approaches. In an American context, as the risk associated with failure grows, managers tend to hedge their bets by involving bottom-up opinions. Similarly, an over-conservative Japanese manager might never show a significant achievement without taking individual initiative.)

The American quality movement was born in industrial organizations as an extension of shop-floor engineering efforts. It is not surprising that the TQM language is anchored in engineering and scientific principles. Even when considering intangible human resources, the tendency is to take a scientific, rational view and look for the best way.

Furthermore, formal strategic planning was introduced to improve competitive performance as organizations grew and became increasingly complex. Formal strategic planning determined the objectives and strategies governing resource allocation and met the organization's mission. Using formal planning to improve the organization's quality implied that the firm's quality-related initiatives must adhere to explicitly formalized procedures.

As I shared these perspectives with my teams, we were better able to consider our approach options, decide on the best courses of action, and experience greater success and unity in purpose in achieving the desired company outcomes.

Consider now which approach (or what combination of both)—tortoise or hare—might work best in personal and relationship objectives. Principles of Quality Control contain many secrets that can be applied not only to industry and business, but life goals as well.

Fun-Ditty #4.1

> "Seven Deadly Sins: wealth without work, pleasure without conscience, knowledge without character, commerce without morality, science without humanity, worship without sacrifice, politics without principle."
>
> – Mohandas K. Gandhi

4.2 – Statistics, Why? – A Profound Secret!

Statistical Thinking relates to how people process information (learning) and respond to it (action). It is based on the premise that Variation exists in all processes. That is always true, a fact of life!

Dr. Walter A. Shewhart of Bell Telephone Laboratories developed a theory in the 1920s where he identified two components of variation; a steady component and an intermittent component. The first, called common or random variation, is caused by chance or undiscovered causes. It occurs randomly. Intermittent variation, the second type, results from assignable causes (causes we can discover). We can only eliminate common cause variation by changing the system. Attempts to do so will always increase the common variation.

So, where (how) can we use this? Volatility is with us! Using statistics gives us control, providing the means to deal with volatility and improve industrial processes. A savvy tech will look at volatility and see opportunity.

Statistics is truly a philosophy of learning and action, distinctly separating statistical *thinking* (a set of thought processes) from *number-crunching* (the use of particular statistical tools). In every walk of life, we find variations. So, how can we deal with variations rationally?

As young technicians, we were taught that when we needed to know how big something was, we just went out and measured it. Then we knew! But we then learned if we made the exact measurement later, the measured value was always different. Then we weren't so sure. But the fact is, no matter how hard we try to hold all variables constant and exercise the greatest caution to repeat all measurements in precisely the same way, there will nonetheless be variability in the measurements. If we don't find a difference, we aren't measuring close enough. That is reality.

Therefore, in the face of variation and the resulting uncertainty, we must develop ways to deal with data. For instance, what do we use for a product dimension in our literature when the results differ for two units from the same production lot? How do we define the "average" of measured data? In one case, the variation may be slight, while in another case quite extreme. How do we quantify the level of variation?

Lord Kelvin said it best over a hundred years ago:

> "When you can measure what you are speaking about, and can express it in numbers, you know something about it; but when you cannot measure

> *it, when you cannot express it in numbers, your knowledge is of a meager and unsatisfactory kind."*

So, unless we can measure what we are dealing with, we are poor technologists. Quantifying data is the basis of descriptive statistics, describing how data is to be viewed and deriving information from that data.

To illustrate this point, consider for a moment what mental images are invoked by just hearing or reading different words. What comes to your mind as you read these terms?

MELLOW SATIN AUTUMN CRÈME

Don't those words feel good? How about:

EXAMINATION CROAK STATISTICS

"Statistics" has never been a popular word. It just does not conjure up warm fuzzies in most people's minds. There are a few good reasons for such a negative image. Taxation and military service were the earliest uses of statistics and let governments know how far they could go into our pocketbooks. Advertising has also abused statistics, causing us to distrust much of what we see. When an ad suggests "Nine out of ten…" they want us to believe that it means "Nine out of EVERY ten…."

Our approach to the science of statistics, however, will be very positive. We will start with the definition: "Statistics is a set of rules allowing us to get and present information from the data."

The fact is, we can easily find ourselves overwhelmed with numbers (data). But *data* is not *information*. It has been said that data lives forever, but information has a very short half-life. Therefore, we must efficiently and promptly turn data into information to make decisions.

Since variation is always present when we observe things in the real world, we MUST practice statistics. The question is not *whether* we should, but *how*. I discovered during my career that ignorance of statistical techniques in today's competitive marketplace can be catastrophic!

Descriptive Statistics

It's one thing to get comfortable with the importance of statistics. It's an entirely different thing to know how to utilize them. If you gather statistics without knowing which kinds will be useful to you, you can draw the wrong conclusions and make costly mistakes. To illustrate this point, it's important to understand *descriptive* statistics.

Descriptive statistics describe the characteristics of a *population* with numerical measurements called *parameters*. With the right parameters, there is no uncertainty, because *all* elements in a population will be considered. To do this, the first task is to define the population. While descriptive statistics are essential, used incorrectly they can also create difficulties.

For example, if the population we measure is the *average family*, how do we define *family*, and how would we define *average*? Further, data gathering can add more difficulties even if the population is clearly defined.

"Average" Loses Information!

One inherent problem with using an average to define anything can be illustrated by this example:

> Fire at a duck. If the 1st shot goes to the right, and 2nd the shot goes to the left, on *average*, the duck should be dead, but it's not. It just flies away.

As another case for the need for descriptive statistics, *illegal aliens* are a well-defined population but a tough place to collect information. The gathering of data has caused many projects to go down the tube. Yet, the importance and value of data gathering and correct statistical analysis cannot be overemphasized. Memories can fail us; therefore, we need data! We forget things, especially those which are unfavorable. Besides, we can only say we know how things will behave if we remember how they acted previously!

Information contained in descriptive statistical data is easiest to see and understand when it can be shown in a picture graphically. A simple graph will show the essential characteristics:

CENTRAL TENDENCY
(or location, measured as the average or mean)
DISPERSION (spread or how much variability)
SHAPE (how the dispersion in the data is located)

The importance of choosing the right "shape" for displaying the data can be shown with an example from the Denver housing market. Several years ago, the demographics (statistics of the area) found the average family size to be 1.8 children. Three-bedroom homes were built accordingly but failed to sell as planned. Millions of dollars were spent on unoccupied houses.

Studies found the population was made up of two distributions: a large segment of young working couples who didn't have or want children and another segment of large families with four or more children. The average was correct, and the variability was alright, but the shape had been neglected.

In other cases, even one number can help give us a picture of the population. For example, do you know what a "Sydney Duck" is? Would you have a better idea about its population if you knew the average weight is 165 pounds? Data may contain information just crying to be noticed, but we must learn to listen and ask the right questions. We must gain an appreciation for and abilities in "listening skills."

Frequency Distributions

In the science of statistics, a picture is worth a thousand words (or numbers). The image most often used for data distribution is called a Frequency Histogram or Frequency Distribution. Data is arranged according to size, spotlighting where most data is grouped, and the pattern of variation.

> *Had a Histogram been used in the Denver housing example mentioned earlier, millions of dollars could have been saved.*

What we learn from this is that a histogram is the *best* way to measure the third characteristic in descriptive statistics (the shape of the distribution).

To illustrate this type of statistical graphic, suppose we place a large spinner with a pointer on a board and let the random variable X be the pointer's position, as shown below. If we place small marks with the numbers 1 through 10 evenly spaced around the board next to each dividing line, what is the chance (probability) that the pointer will stop exactly on, say, the line marked 5? Virtually ZERO! The pointer could get close to the 5 (or any other number), but to stop *precisely* on one of the lines would be extremely unlikely.

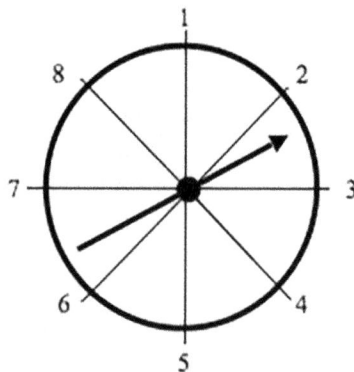

On the other hand, if we divide that same circle into eight equal *segments* as shown in the next image, with the number 5 representing the space *between the lines,* or one-eighth of the total circle, the probability of the pointer landing on the number 5 is now 1 spin out of 8 = 1/8 = 0.125.

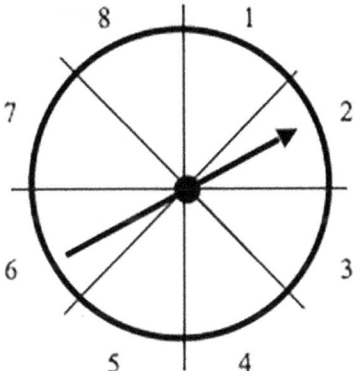

Notice the sum of all segments, or the area of the total figure is ONE! (or unity) – 100% of all outcomes – that means the outcomes under the diagram must include all trials. All possible outcomes are included.

The lesson here is that you can only assign probability to RANGES. This can be a powerful perspective if you think about what this can imply, not just in industry, but also in life. As you strive to achieve ideal objectives, consider fixating less on exact outcomes, and more on a range of experiences or results that could accomplish the desired satisfaction.

Fun-Ditty #4.2

"The one thing I know: the only ones among you who will be really happy are those who have sought and found how to serve."

– Albert Schweitzer

4.3 — The Joseph Juran Secret(s)

Deming (mentioned earlier), first taught the math of *control*. He then told the Japanese they needed to talk to his friend Dr. Juran, who came in and taught *improvement* (the management side of the coin). Juran published his Quality Control Handbook in 1951, which the Japanese got hold of and asked, who is Juran? It would be a ten-year investment by Quality Managers before they saw any success.

When I started to work for Standard Microsystems in New York, I was blessed to sit through a two-week presentation by Dr. Joseph Juran, considered the father of Quality Control. What I learned in that 80-hour course propelled me to a higher-level understanding and grasp of all things quality!

About Dr. Juran:

> *Dr. Juran wrote many books and traveled the world, training top leaders in quality control concepts. He created a trilogy for managing quality based on Planning, Control, and Improvement. He fathered the idea of applying the Pareto principle to reducing defects, that 80% of the problems come from 20% of the causes. In addition, he asserts the number one cause of almost all problems is "resistance to change." (See https://www.quality-assurance-solutions.com/Joseph-Moses-Juran.html)*

He said poor quality costs us in four ways: Prevention, Appraisal, Internal-failure, and External-failure. Rather than talk of the cost of *quality*, it makes more sense to talk of the costs of *poor quality*. Each of these four categories must be targeted for us to compete in the global marketplace.

Problem-Solving

Dr. Juran broke problem-solving into two journeys, the diagnostic and the remedial. He suggested the first is more important, because too little time is spent defining the problem. After all, it is necessary to choose the method before starting the journey. If we are planning to cross a river, do we need to build a bridge, cross in a boat, or can we leap across without the help of any structure?

Once diagnosed, the remedy is usually mechanical. In other words, once the plan has been identified, carrying it out can typically be done without additional thought. We can provide a better product at a lower cost ahead of the need, with a smile!

In the diagnosis phase, we must anticipate what our customers will want or need before starting the journey. But some of our widest and most treacherous rivers are not yet apparent to our customers. Therefore, many "what if?" queries about "good, cheap, fast, and happy" need to be made to improve our competitive position.

Dr. Juran further explained that problems often go unheeded for fear of being swept away in undercurrents or whitewater, never reaching the other side. *Problems* refer to both special and common causes of variation. We must work on making "unstable processes stable, stable but incapable processes capable, and capable processes yet more capable." (See http://qualityshabbir.tripod.com/Articles/Deming14.htm)

Ultimately, problems are opportunities for improvement. If we don't find the problems, they will surely find us. So, how appropriate are these observations as we attempt to improve a production process? Everyone's job should not merely be to 'do it right' but to 'do it better.'

Financial Management vs. Quality Management

Financial management uses three stages, and any quality operation that does not include all three stages will fail. These stages are:

1. Financial planning,
2. Financial control (cost control, expense control), and
3. Financial improvement.

Dr. Juran taught that Management for Quality uses the *same* three processes – what he called The Quality Trilogy :

1. Planning (where the customer determines product needs and requirements),
2. Control (developing the means to satisfy customer needs and requirements), and
3. Improvement (the most crucial feature of the trilogy).

This Quality concept in fact applies to all industries, functions, and processes. We note that once the planning is complete, there is no clear responsibility for improvement. The operating forces take over, but their job is quality control, not quality improvement. This severe lack of foresight must be corrected.

So, how have so many companies made such improvements? Resounding feedback is that they did it by establishing a new organizational structure and managerial processes designed to create new advancements in quality.

However, middle managers already have formal, legitimate goals, budgets, specifications, and quotas. Vagueness cannot compete with structure and legitimacy.

Dr. Juran counseled that three things are essential from the management position so that they fully empowered the workforce with:

1) Clear written statements of what is expected of the employee,
2) A clear understanding of how each employee is doing against those expectations, and
3) The ability to change any difference between 1 and 2.

Management must insist on these three things from an employer to make their maximum contribution. More about Dr. Juran and his teachings are in the Notes for this Chapter.

These principles made a powerful impact in industry and manufacturing, but they can also be applied in families and other organizations. Do we communicate expectations clearly, and revisit those expectations with a vision for continuing improvement?

Fun-Ditty #4.3

> *"Education is the ability to listen to almost anything without losing your temper or your self-confidence."*
> *– Robert Frost*

4.4 – Living Behind the Quality Dikes

Before industrialization, the great mass of humanity lived in villages with primitive conditions of transport, communication, energy sources, health care, Etc. Life was short and exhausting, with much poverty, disease, and hunger.

With the industrial revolution, hundreds of millions of people could now take advantage of central energy sources, modern transport, communication, improved health, longer life, reduced toil, the opportunity for travel, time for cultural activities, etc. These are all important benefits, but they have generated a dependence that our forefathers did not have to worry about regarding the Quality of manufactured products and services.

We take this dependence for granted, but it is very serious indeed. For instance, in the U.S., over 80% of the workforce used privately owned vehicles for transportation to the workplace. If the vehicle fails, the motorist cannot walk to work–they no longer live within walking distance of their work. When the auto fails, we must arrange for some alternative.

Dr. Juran described our dependence on quality as much like the Dutch living behind quality dikes. About one-third of their lands lie below sea level. The land provides great benefits, but using it requires massive sea walls to be built and maintained to keep the seawater out. Likewise, modern products and services provide great benefits but also demand protective dikes in the form of adequate quality controls.

Why should anyone take such a risk? One explanation is that we merely have a passion for excellence. That is why some see a mountain as an obstacle; others see it as something to be climbed. This passage describes the reason well:

"A passion for excellence means thinking big and starting small: excellence happens when high purpose and intense pragmatism meet. This is almost, but not quite, the whole truth. We believe a passion for excellence also carries a price, and we state it simply: the adventure of excellence is not for the faint of heart. Adventure? You bet. It's not just a job. It's a personal commitment.

"Whether we're looking at a billion-dollar corporation or a three-person accounting department, we see that excellence is achieved by people who muster up the nerve (and the passion) to step out—in spite of doubt, or fear, or job description—to maintain face-to-face contact with other people, namely customers and colleagues. They won't retreat behind office doors, committees, memos or layers of staff, knowing this is the fair bargain they make for extraordinary results. They may step out for love, because of a burning desire to be the best, to make a difference, or perhaps, as a colleague recently explained, 'because the thought of being average scares the hell out of me.'" (Peters & Austin. A Passion for Excellence: The Leadership Difference, New York, Random House. 1985)

Leadership

Effectively Quality Control requires good leadership, and a good leader must have infectious optimism. The greatest test for a leader is how you feel when leaving his presence after a conference. Do you feel uplifted and confident?

Good leaders believe in people. They believe all people will contribute if given a chance. Members can be ordered to come to work five days a week to work their full shift, but they cannot be ordered to perform in an excellent fashion. Excellence, by its definition at all levels, is a purely voluntary commitment. It will happen only if the job is sincerely "owned."

A passionate response by Ren McPherson, former chairman of the Data Corporation and one of the truly great industrial leaders of our time, was made when a Consultant told him what he should do with "his" people, "…No! No! No! Do not do this or that for your people! They aren't 'your people.' You don't own 'em. Don't you see?"

Another reason for establishing very close customer contact relates to perceptions of product quality. The customer (user) is only concerned with fitness for use; that is, does the product do what it is supposed to do?

On the other hand, the manufacturer is only concerned with conformance to spec at the final test. Is it ever possible that these two perceptions of quality do not match? We must be close enough to the customer to know how well conformance to specs at the final test complies with the customer's perception of fitness for use. Quality is what the customer says he needs, not what our tests indicate is satisfactory. (See *The Warning Signs, A Pop Quiz on Quality* - Robelle. http://www.robelle.com/library/papers/popquiz/)

In short, we must be sure that customer perceptions are a valued input to the quality program. Become obsessed with listening! Get out from behind the desk to where the customers are, hang out on their turf, and listen "naively" and intensely, providing fast feedback on quick action.

Fun-Ditty #4.4

> *"Excellent companies do not believe in excellence –*
> *only in constant improvement and constant change."*
> *- Tom Peters*

4.5 – Intuition

Most of us have been pulled or pushed through an educational system that has cherished language, numbers, sequential thinking, logic, and verbal memories (all left-brain stuff). What has been neglected is the non-verbal, non-number, non-obvious part of our brain.

How about intuition? How about the gut feeling of a situation? How about the visual "aha!" that comes when we understand an issue when that light seems to go on?

Great achievers always visualize their goals before they set out to achieve them. The methods to get there often appear as hunches and intuition. True breakthroughs in any field usually originate in the right brain. Albert Einstein said, "The really valuable thing is intuition."

We have mistakenly been led to believe that words and numbers equate to human intelligence. We now know that is only half the answer. As demonstrated earlier, people often respond more readily to visual stimuli than verbal ones.

The right brain plays a decisive role in how we approach problems. Split-brain patients are missing communication between the left and right brains but it is so vital to the work we do. We can observe it, but we can't explain it. We know it goes on but do not know why. We call it intuition, and it must be used in our approach to solving industrial problems.

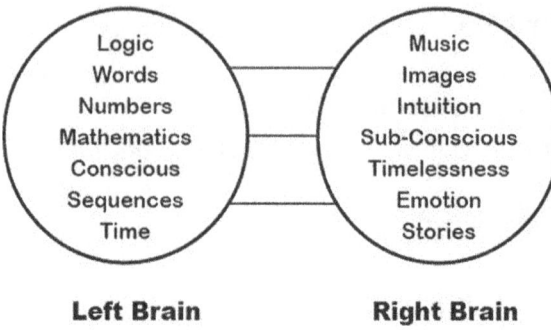

Left Brain   **Right Brain**

A problem-solving paradigm I used for many years before understanding the connection between the two-brain approach is as follows:

1) Orientation: Define the problem in its total context.
2) Over-preparation: Study, read, interview, experiment, and do everything possible to load the left brain with information about the problem and all its implications. Overwhelm the left brain with details relating to the problem.
3) Incubation: Drop the whole thing for a period, a day, a night and a day, a week, an hour, whatever is available, and let the left brain communicate with the image-processing right brain.
4) Illumination: Enjoy the ideas that flow into your consciousness, the insights, and the intuition that provides pictures of unheard-of solutions.

A defect in the traditional left-brain thinking process is the notion that there is only one answer or only one best solution to a problem. That notion limits our ability to solve both industrial problems, and life problems. The image processor on the right side of our brain can bring to our attention many otherwise overlooked possibilities. These ideas may seem off-the-wall, but they can as often provide insight otherwise missed.

> *Engaging both sides of our brain and entertaining "What if" thinking effectively stimulates a greater flow of ideas and helps us discover more permanent and lasting solutions to various problems.*

Each of these ideas fascinated me, and captivated my students during my assignment in New York. Eventually, my wife and I found ourselves with an empty nest, and though I continued teaching quality control for the chip manufacturer there, we ultimately (but not permanently) settled in Cleveland, Ohio. While in Ohio, I joined a group that was trying to capitalize on the crash of the Soviet Union and the chance to market quality US goods at attractive prices.

What that meant for my wife and me was another expat experience, but this time working to elevate Russian product quality to US standards.

Fun-Ditty #4.5

> *"The greatest obstacle to discovering the shape of the earth, the continents, and the oceans was not ignorance, but the illusion of knowledge."*
> — *Daniel J. Boorstin*

NOTES ON CHAPTER 4

Thinking Out of the Box

The following question is said to have appeared on a physics degree exam at the University of Copenhagen, reportedly posted in the "Engineers Weekly" publication of Denmark:

> "Describe how to determine the height of a skyscraper with a barometer."

One enterprising student replied: "You tie a long piece of string to the neck of the barometer, then lower the barometer from the roof of the skyscraper to the ground. The length of the string plus the length of the barometer will equal the height of the building."

This highly original answer so incensed the examiner that the student failed immediately. The student appealed because his answer was indisputably correct, and the university appointed an independent arbiter to decide the case.

The arbiter judged that the answer was correct but failed to display any noticeable knowledge of physics. To resolve the problem, it was decided to allow the student six minutes to verbally provide an answer that showed at least a minimal familiarity with the basic principles of physics.

For five minutes, the student sat silently, forehead creased in thought. The arbiter reminded him that time was running out. The student replied that he had several relevant answers but couldn't decide which to use.

On being advised to hurry up, the student replied as follows:

"Firstly, you could take the barometer up to the roof of the skyscraper, drop it over the edge, and measure the time it takes to drop to the ground. The height of the building can then be worked out from the formula H = 1/2 gt squared (height equals half times gravity times time squared), but bad luck for the barometer.

Or, if the sun is shining, you could measure the height of the barometer, then set it on its end and measure the length of its shadow. Then you measure the length of the skyscraper's shadow. After that, it is a simple matter of proportional arithmetic to work out the skyscraper's height. Suppose you merely wanted to be boring and orthodox about it. In that case, you could use the barometer to measure the air pressure on the skyscraper's roof, compare it with standard air pressure on the ground, and convert the difference in mili-bars into feet in order to give the height of the building.

However, since we're constantly being urged to exercise independence of mind and apply scientific methods, the best way would be to knock on the janitor's door and say to him, 'I will give you this nice new barometer if you will tell me the height of this skyscraper.'"

The arbiter re-graded the student with an 'A.'

Variations of this story have also been told in the following publications:

- Canfield, Jack. Chicken Soup for the College Soul. Health Communications, 1999.

- van der Linden, Peter. Expert C Programming. Englewood Cliffs, NJ: Prentice Hall, 1994.
- The Big Book of Urban Legends. New York: Paradox Press, 1994.

More on DOE

The reason and purpose for DOE can be shown with a simple experiment on how to test a simple wire-bond process. We did that at Intel, Motorola, and now at SMC.

The process of connecting wires to terminals inside an integrated circuit (IC) is shown below. The tool places the wire against the first bond pad, secured (welded) by a burst of ultrasonic energy, then the tool is opened, pulling the wire out as it moves over to the second pad, repeating the bond to the second pad, then closing on the wire to break it off and pull it away from the package.

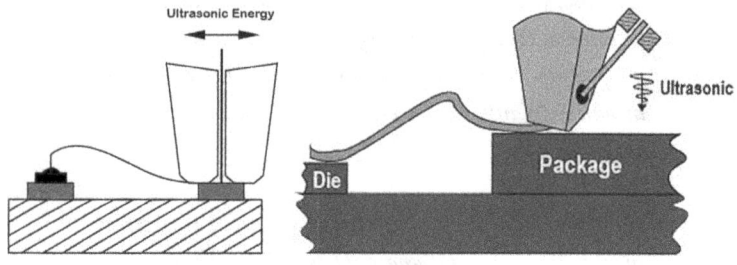

This process, done automatically, and controlled by a computer, moves through the geometry of the IC with blinding speed. But how do we know if it was a successful operation? Similar automation tests a sample of the connections by pulling them to the breaking point to see if the bond produced was strong enough. Some sample size, conforming to the spec, says yea or nay. If sufficient bond pulls are within spec, the lot is passed.

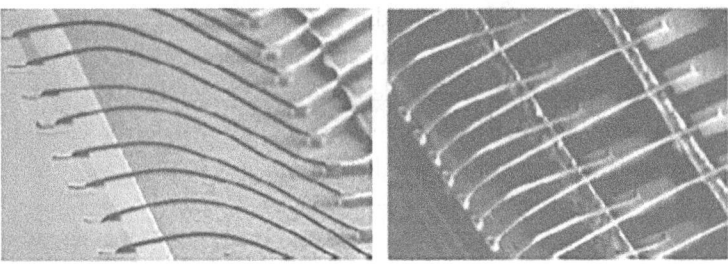

To punch up the importance of DOE, consider the following two-variable process shown in Fig. 16.3: The output (Z) is some function of X and Y. Or, given the coordinates of X and Y, the output, Z, is identified by the function illustrated here:

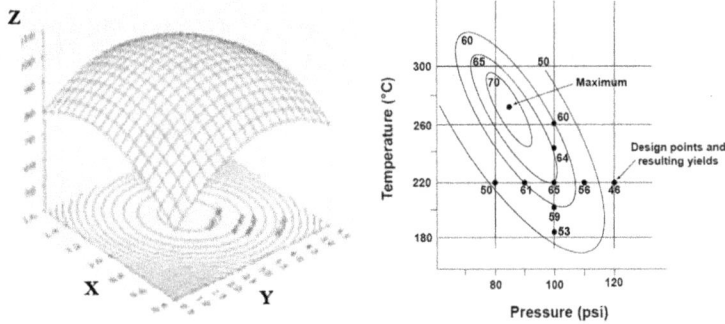

Two factors are thought to influence the yield of a chemical process (Temperature and Pressure). We aim to find the best combinations of these two factors for the highest process yield. Let's see what the process tells us if we approach this task one factor at a time. Fix the temperature, say at 220 degrees. Then change pressure, conducting experiments at different pressure levels, say at 80, 90, 100, 110, and 120 psi. Identify the pressure that maximizes yield. Graphically, the optimum pressure is 100 psi.

Then leave the pressure at this value, 100 psi, and change the temperature above and below the default starting point at 180, 200, 220, 240, and 260. The conclusion that maximum yield occurs at 100 psi and about 220 degrees is wrong. Of course, we could continue iterating one factor at a time toward better conditions, but it would be painfully slow and expensive. Changing one factor at a time didn't work here!

A better approach uses a designed experiment (DOE), with a factorial arrangement, for two factors, two levels. What does it tell us? It tells us which way to move for higher performance values.

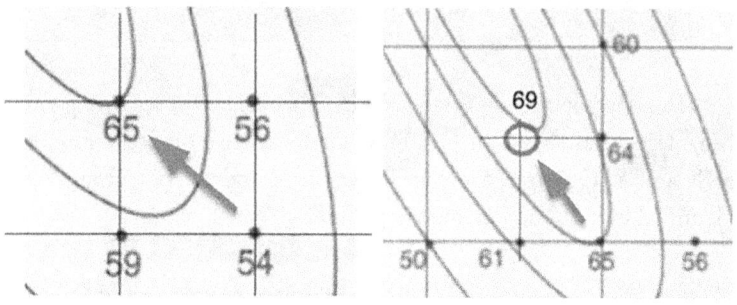

Factor DOE, and Higher yield, with one additional data point

More on Quality

The TWO journeys to eliminate waste:

    Diagnostic Journey: From Symptom to Cause
    Remedial Journey: From Cause to Remedy

The THREE phases of maturity:

    <u>Dependence</u> –
    "You take care of me…
    "You came through for me…
    "I blame you…

    <u>Independence</u> –
    "I can do it…
    "I am responsible…
    "I can choose…

Interdependence –
"We can do it…
"We can cooperate…
"We can combine our talents to…

As Stephen R. Covey taught: "Interdependence is a choice only independent people can make," and "Trust is the highest form of human motivation."

So I learned to ask myself (and challenge my teams with) the question: Are you here with a solution? Or are you part of the problem?

There are two kinds of delegation.

1) "Gofer – Go for this and that and tell me when it's done."
2) "Stewardship – Give people a choice and make them responsible for the results."

Efficiency: Doing things right, vs
Effectiveness: Doing the right things.

Which is more important??? Remember Aesop's goose with the golden eggs? We must consider both the P and the PC. P = Production (getting the result), and PC = Production Capability – the ability or asset that produces the golden eggs.

Most people see effectiveness from the Golden Egg paradigm: The more you produce, the more you do, and the more effective you are. But true effectiveness is a function of what is produced (the golden eggs) and the producing asset or capacity to produce (the goose). (What is True Effectiveness? Considering balance in life …. https://paulineharley.medium.com/what-is-true-effectiveness-86a67533f25f)

If you adopt a pattern of life that focuses on the eggs and neglects the goose, you will soon be without the asset that produces the golden eggs. (The Goose and the Golden egg principle - Speaking Tree. https://www.speakingtree.in/blog/the-goose-and-the-golden-egg-principle)

On the other hand, if you only take care of the goose, you soon won't be able to feed the goose or yourself. (Effectiveness Defined - Leadership. https://ucieserve.wordpress.com/the-seven-habits/effectiveness-defined/)

More About the Hare Approach:

According to the planning paradigm for quality, the quality improvement process begins with an organization's quality vision and definition (the organization's strategic leaders generally conceive it). Next, quality plans are formulated with a detailed assessment of organizational strengths and weaknesses and benchmarking of the external environment on the other.

These quality plans (action plans) are controlled by the organization's quality supervisors and managers, who define tactical quality targets. The action plans are handed down to the front-line quality workers for implementation. According to Frederick Taylor, the planning and implementation functions are divided and entrusted to managers and workers.

The strategic leader or planner plays a critical role in this planning model. Many believe that a critical requirement for an organization's quality improvement effort is the active involvement of top management. Commitment by top management (and sometimes threats) sustains the interest of other employees.

There is a tendency by many hands-on leaders, however, not to relinquish control. They take over the day-to-day quality action plans and insist on overseeing their implementation. Such intentions, noble as they might seem, could distract the leaders from monitoring and adapting the organization's strategic direction in an ever-changing environment.

Under this top-down planning paradigm, managers and workers are expected to adhere completely to the direction set by top managers. Senior management dictates, explicitly or implicitly: "My way or the highway." Legitimate differences of opinion are construed as opposition to quality principles and can lead to a quick dismissal.

More on the Spinner Experiment:

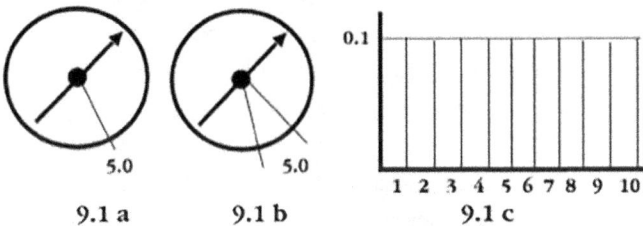

Distribution of Spinner Results

The circle's frequency distribution (probability density) would look like this, with the height of each bar equal to 0.1. Notice the sum of all bars, or the area of the total figure, is ONE! One hundred percent of all outcomes, or the area under the diagram, must include all trials. There is no possible outcome that is not included in the figure. The likelihood in 9.1(a) of the pointer stopping exactly on 5.0 is next to Zero. In Fig. 9(b), each segment equals 1/10 of the total picture. Here, the chance of landing on any segment equals 1/10 or 0.1. The histogram Fig. 9.1(c) sums up the likelihood of all events nicely.

More on the Juran Secrets:

In applying our knowledge of cause-and-effect relationships, we examine: what happened and why, what could happen, and what the future might hold. Unfortunately, the future holds less urgency than the present. This largely remains an unfulfilled potential; the ability to plan and take action against the negative events of tomorrow.

Some structure is essential to get the maximum contribution of relevant information from several people working on one problem. It is also essential that people understand each other's words. You have probably seen this little sign on an office wall or desk: "I know that you believe you understood what you thought I said, but what I said is not what I meant!"

Many companies, proud of their product quality, rigidly enforce a quality policy that requires rigorous product inspections, immediate process shutdowns, and 100% sorting when problems are detected.

When management accepts this policy, they expect the lines to be shut down often to protect their image as a high-quality supplier. They naturally accept the costs required for a team of inspectors to ensure high outgoing quality. Since management knows that customers' delivery schedules must be met, they approve of the high cost of adequate work-in-process inventories to buffer the shutdowns.

Additional personnel are required to make mid-course changes, including schedulers, material expediters, machine changeover people, process engineering troubleshooters, and additional production supervisors. The additional management staff is also required to deal with unpredictable production operations.

Tampering with a stable process increases variability. But what is a stable process? One with no variability? Action taken on a stable system in response to variation within the control limits to compensate for this variation is tampering. This holds even if a stable system is producing faulty items. A faulty item is not a signal of a special cause. Watch trends well within specs, allowing adjustments before a bad product is produced. (https://studylib.net/doc/8605556/lessons-learned-from-the-red-bead-experiment)

It is impossible to have zero variability. That is why we have tolerances on specifications. For instance, if the aim of a dimension is 20 mm, the design specification might say 20 +/- .03 mm. This would tell the manufacturing department that, while it should aim for 20 mm, anything between 19.97 and 20.03 is all right. The signal, in this case, is 20, and the noise is +/- 0.03.

Engineers are taught deterministic methods and sheltered from the reality of variation. One such example, documented by Genichi Taguchi, concerns the power supply design. Taguchi reported that the initial design of a power supply, which consisted of 13 active components, put the output voltage at the specified setpoint of 115 but with a standard deviation of 12 volts. Using the methods involving the S/N just described, the variation was reduced to only one volt without upgrading the components' tolerances. In other words, in this 13-variable function, the DOE could put the voltage characteristic on target with low variation and do so at less cost within a short development time.

Attacking the causes of product variation requires a change of practices that extends far beyond the operator's realm into every function and level of the organization. The leadership, investment of resources, and change of organizational systems required to achieve sustained improvement in all business areas, including production, cannot be accomplished by anyone except managers. It is often difficult to convince managers that they should lead and participate in quality improvement.

Many managers do not see the effect of quality on the traditional internal measures of business performance (cost, throughput, performance to schedule, equipment utilization, etc.). Each measure is usually evaluated separately from all others. Sometimes there appears to be limited understanding of the measures' interrelationships and mutual dependence on the quality of daily work that goes on in the entire organization. Without the active participation of every individual in the organization, including leaders, requiring improvements will probably not be sufficient for long-term survival.

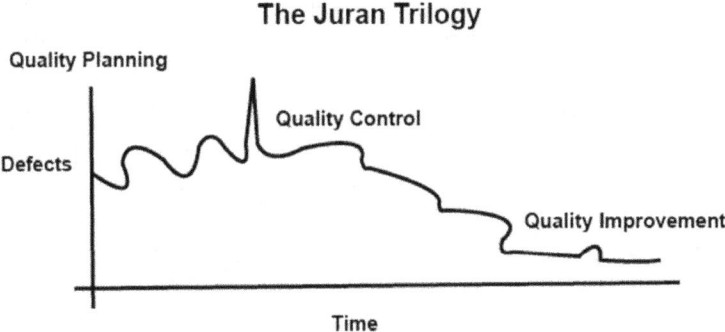

The 3rd process in the trilogy is Quality Improvement. Identify specific projects for improvement, organize project teams, discover causes, develop remedies, prove effectiveness of remedies, deal with cultural resistance, establish controls to hold the gains, then, do it all over again!

Upper managers lacked working knowledge about how to manage quality. [Ready, fire, aim] To make a wise choice of strategy, managers need knowledge about how to manage quality.

(See: Juran, J.M.. Juran on Quality by Design, Simon and Schuster. Free Press, May 4, 1992)

More on Living Behind the Quality Dikes

In today's marketplace, the ability to change rapidly, to reduce the design/prototype phase of new product development will be the key to success. Statistical techniques are essential in this measurement process to get the maximum amount of information from the available data. Statistics should be viewed as important tools to help collect and present data to evaluate current theories and form new theories. In other words, statistics help us learn.

Major management efforts must be aimed at making non-stop small improvements that inch productivity along. Process breakthroughs are welcomed, but real success comes from what has been described as incremental improvements in mature technologies.

The only way to ensure 100% usable purchased parts and materials from vendors is to teach them the value of quality planning, quality improvement, and quality control. This cannot be dictated via purchase requirements but only through long-term partnerships and a handshake mentality as members of the same team. This will include accurately defined specifications for the vendors to deal with, involved early in the design cycle, with adequate quality index targets. It must also include levels of trust and flexibility, allowing the vendor to use his resources best. A teamwork effort of this sort must communicate to all suppliers the detail and extent of company expectations.

Buyers/Seller's Risk

When we build anything, we ask the question: Did it turn out as intended? Or, more simply, did it meet spec? Whether it's the diameter of a piston, the weight of a bolt of cloth, the percentage of sugar in a soft drink, or the length of a straw, there are always two outcomes: Yes or no!

But asking that question has four possible answers:

1. Yes, it meets spec (and it really does)
2. No, it doesn't meet spec (and it really doesn't)
3. Yes, we say it meets spec (but it doesn't), and
4. No, we reject the product (when it's really ok).

Science calls these Type 1 and Type 2 errors.

> If I reject the belief and scrap the part when it is good,
> I've committed a Type 1 error.
> SELLERS RISK! Bad for the seller – Type 1 Error

> If I accept the belief and ship the part when it is bad,
> I've committed a Type II error.
> BUYERS RISK! Bad for the buyer – Type 2 Error

Data collection is gathering and measuring information on targeted variables in an established system, enabling one to answer relevant questions and evaluate outcomes. Data collection is a component of research in all fields of study, including physical and social sciences, humanities, and business. While methods vary by discipline, the emphasis on ensuring accurate and honest collection remains the same. The goal for all data collection is to capture quality evidence that allows analysis to formulate convincing and credible answers to the questions that have been posted. (Data collection - Wikipedia. https://en.wikipedia.org/wiki/Data_collection_plan) how do we assess

A perfect test would have zero false positives and zero false negatives. (Type I and type II errors - Wikipedia. https://en.wikipedia.org/wiki/Type_I_and_type_II_errors)

However, statistics is a game of probability, and it cannot be known whether statistical conclusions are correct. Whenever there is uncertainty, there is the possibility of making an error. Considering the nature of statistics in science, all statistical hypothesis tests will likely make type I and II errors.

- The type I error rate or significance level is the probability of rejecting the null hypothesis, given that it is true. It is denoted by the Greek letter α (alpha) and is also called the alpha level. Usually, the significance level is set to 0.05 (5%), implying that it is acceptable to have a 5% probability of incorrectly rejecting the true null hypothesis.
- The rate of the type II error is denoted by the Greek letter β (beta) and related to the power of a test, which equals $1-\beta$.

These two types of error rates are traded against each other. Reducing one type of error generally increases the other type for any given sample set. (https://indiafreenotes.com/statistical-errors-and-approximation/)

CHAPTER 5

Russia

5.0 — Creation of Synchron

Russia Part 1

In 1993, I joined a small consulting group, hoping to capitalize on Russian manufacturing capability, currently underutilized with the recent collapse of the Soviet Union. Additionally, this was a time when low raw materials cost provided added incentive. Our company began as Synchron, Inc., with one president, four VPs, and one clerk (the President's wife, Sue).

We met in Florida to kick off this venture. Our goal: Find Russian companies to manufacture products popular in the west for mutual economic benefit. For example, low-end printers marketed through Xerox, automotive brake parts sold through Lucas Brake Systems (Great Britain), etc. Steve Griffiths, our President, has had many years of experience with Booz-Allen consulting and other high-level connections. One of our VPs, Ilya Kogan, was a Russian expat with wider (wilder) ideas than all beliefs. Maurice Nobert (a peer manager at Intel from back in the day) and Ed McCarthy rounded out our team of six. I was the quality guy for the effort.

Steve's experience with Booz-Allen was our connection with potential global entities. The Booz mantra is taking on clients' complex problems at the intersection of technology and mission, focused on innovation to constantly press the boundaries of what is possible. The talent and dedication of the people of Booz-Allen formed the foundation of its success. Incidentally, Booz was named "the world's most profitable spy organization." According to an Information Week piece from 2002, Booz-Allen had "more than one thousand former intelligence officers on its staff."

My Russian task began in February 1994, flying from Cleveland, Ohio, to St. Petersburg, Russia. My coworkers Ilya and Ed had met in Moscow a few weeks earlier, setting the stage for future business connections.

I learned that St. Petersburg was founded by Peter the Great in 1703. According to the New York Times, its name had been changed to "Petrograd" in 1914 at the start of World War I because its original name sounded too German. It was the capital of the Russian Empire until after the Russian Revolution of 1917, when its name was changed to Leningrad. When Communism fell in Russia after WWII, it became St. Petersburg again. It is the second largest city in Europe area-wise (next to London) with over four million people, and is sometimes called the "Venice of Russia".

Though it is only about 300 years old, St. Petersburg is known for its history of dramatic events, gorgeous architecture, and major historical figures. It is one of the most important educational and scientific centers in Russia, with hundreds of research institutes and universities. It is also a major center of engineering, metalwork, tractor and car manufacturing, and shipbuilding.

This beautiful city, rich in history, industry, and culture would be our new home for the next four years. What I wasn't fully prepared for were the particular challenges of bringing quality control practices into environments where baseline ethical standards and values were very much different from what I had been accustomed to in the West.

My First Russian Visit

Booz-Allen was working with a steel company in St. Petersburg (Stoomhammer) LZTL, with limited success. Steve had agreed to help with their effort and asked me to spend a few weeks on that job to support the Booz engineer, Ed Frey.

The LZTL factory was in trouble since their Russian market had almost dried up. Only some of the managers accepted the Booz initiative. Others were openly hostile.

We were picked up at the hotel at 7:30 on our first day. We then traveled about 35 minutes across the city to the plant. We got back to the hotel at about 7:30 in the evening. The days were really short there, so it was mostly in the dark. The water in the plant was surely not for drinking. When you flushed the toilet, it left suds in the bowl with a definite color. I drank diet coke there and bottled water at the plant.

Ilya connected me with a Russian technologist, Boris Pavlotsky, to further the Synchron effort in Russia. Boris spoke fluent English, with his native Russian and far-reaching technical connections. So I was to work the Booz job the next day and Thursday, then work with two potential Xerox printer manufacturers with Boris in Moscow on Friday. We were to take a night train (Thursday) to Moscow (a Pullman type with separate compartments) and line up the Synchron effort on Saturday, then go back to St. Petersburg Monday night.

I booked myself into the Commodore Hotel Ship parked in the bay. It was made over as a land-locked floating hotel with all the amenities of a small rooming house, which was much better use of the money!

I finished breakfast, then walked around the ship on the open deck. It was 8:30, and only a little light. The days were short there. There were several people already out on the ice fishing. The fish they caught were only about 3 to 6 inches long, like sardines. But one guy had a small bag filled with them. The people on the ice were friendly even though we didn't communicate.

On the 2nd day back at the Booz job, Joe Metz, the big Booz-Allen guy who was Ed Frey's boss, was in for a few days. That meant we would be busy, busy. I sat through the weekly sales meeting and felt like a Bozo, unaware of what was happening. After the meeting, I made an executive decision and told Ed I couldn't get a handle on it part-time and that I wanted to overwhelm it for two weeks full-time. That would be the two weeks before I flew home.

I went to Moscow on the midnight train Friday night to hold training sessions on Saturday for Synchron. That was the beginning of the Quality Training courses I would deliver in Russia. Then I would ride back to St. Pete Sunday night. I felt good about the decision and looked forward to my time at Booz.

If I were to mention one thing about the Russians: they were smoking themselves to death. Someone said there are two smoking sections, smoking and chain smoking. It had warmed up there; most of the snow was gone from the roads.

As Boris and I were walking from the Trade show in St. Petersburg that week to the hotel, a funny-looking vehicle came across the ice near the bank. A guy climbed out the top and hollered in Russian. Boris talked with him for a while, then Boris invited me to take a ride on the thing, which cost $5.00. The guy was a little scraggly type, about 60, and his vehicle had one giant propeller in the air, and it would cruise about 40 mph just off the ice surface. It was a hoot. The guy had pictures of his trips to the waters (ice) above Siberia and the big mammoth tusks they had found. That was when we stopped and spoke to some of the ice fishermen.

Sunday began on the midnight train to Moscow in St. Petersburg. Ilya and I were helped onto the train by two Russian businessmen interested in Synchron. After about eight hours in Pullman-type sleepers, we pulled into the Moscow train station. We struggled off the train with the Xerox printer and suitcases and were met by Yuri, who put our stuff in a small car.

It was snowing lightly but not too cold as the Russian weather goes. Yuri was a gentleman Ilya met in his Synchron network search. He was retired, formerly a member of the government standards agency who did what we call in the states Source Inspection. He would go to the plants and judge whether the product passed the specifications and if the product could be shipped.

Ilya said this was an important group of people who could support our Synchron effort as it developed. So that was our driver. Ilya felt optimistic about Yuri, 1) he was retired and always available, 2) he had a car, 3) he spoke a little English, and 4) he was genuinely interested in the stuff we were doing. He would like Yuri to be my man in Moscow. I would see.

Ilya said as we packed the stuff into the car, "There is one problem, where to get breakfast!" He made an executive decision to go to Mcdonald's, so away we went. We got there at 9:00, but it didn't open until 10:00, so we got back into the car, and Yuri drove us around the center of the city, pointing out the Kremlin, Red Square, the parliament building (Russian white house) that had been shelled during the last skirmish. Anyway, my first meal in Moscow was a Big Mac. That had been my first meal in Singapore too.

We then made our way to Ilya's apartment, the base of our operations in Moscow. It was a two small bedroom, toilet with bath/shower, and kitchen with a small table on the seventh floor. The elevator held only two people, so Ilya came up after Yuri and I. Ilya called a business contact while I was sending a telegram, who showed up about an hour after we did. We then presented the Synchron pitch, got his comments, and negotiated changes to fit the Russian psyche better.

It was a good session, and Ilya asked if I thought we could use Yuri. I agreed. We would prepare six to ten people for the Certified Quality Engineer exam to serve on our technical search team. Those who made the cut would begin the training/self-education after my trip to the U.S., where I would pull the stuff together and bring it back with me.

Ilya talked to one of his neighbors, Vchyslav, who happens to be, or was, a member of the KGB. His father was a colonel in the secret service. Anyway, he wanted to have dinner with Ilya, drink some vodka and talk about Synchron. Ilya had told him a great deal about the operation. However, Ilya was concerned about Yuri (the driver), who had just brought up a couple of loaves of bread. In Ilya's opinion, Yuri couldn't stand Vchyslav. He was also concerned about my not drinking vodka with this important guest.

I asked Ilya if the guest would be offended if I didn't drink with him. He implied he would but that if he (Ilya) could explain why I didn't drink, it might be ok. I just said it's against my religion! Ilya said that would probably be ok, continuing to mutter, comment, discuss, and consider. I walked away from that discussion and just laid down. It was out of my control.

I dozed a bit, and at about 8:00, Ilya called from the kitchen and said they were waiting for me. So I entered the small kitchen where Vchyslav, Yuri, and Ilya were sitting, ready to dig in. The table was set with stuff that looked like finger food on different dishes. It was apparent one plate was small pieces of some kind of fish. I couldn't guess what was on the other three plates. We started with a potato which I was told had to be peeled.

Vchyslav quickly showed me how to peel a potato and gave me the one he peeled. Ilya explained that one plate was pig fat which they liked to eat when drinking vodka. There was a bottle of vodka on the table. Another plate had cut-up onions in vinegar and oil. Another was a vegetable that tasted pretty good, but nothing I recognized. So I put a few bits of fish, some onions, and a slice of dark bread on my plate with the peeled potato and started to nibble so slowly that it would not look like I needed anything else.

The conversation started, all in fast Russian, about who knows what. Once in a while, Ilya would turn to me and say something like, "…we're talking about Yeltsin's state of the union address…." and away they would go. After other toasts and "we're talking about's…" (Yuri only sipped at his first small glass, never taking a second shot). Vchyslav was beginning to feel no pain, with Ilya somewhere in between, and the dinner went on.

The stuff on the small table would shift when someone moved their elbows. They ate like hungry farmhands, forking a piece of fish, a cube of pig fat, onions, etc., all the while talking a mile a minute. It was interesting to watch their body language and guess what they were talking about. On one occasion, Ilya said they were talking about churches which I assumed since Vchyslav had gone into the posture of praying and crossing himself.

If you can, picture this scene: Yuri was in a red plaid cotton shirt with a paisley tie, Vchyslav wore a nice white shirt and tie (a rough Kirk Douglas type about my age) and did most of the talking, but not a word of English, just a big grin all the time, and Ilya (like Danny DeVito, only a little more obnoxious, with a short beard) stabbing food across the table.

After dinner, Ilya did the Russian hitchhiker thing, and he and I were on the road in about two minutes. The hitchhiker goes like this: You simply step into the street and put your hand out like you are pointing at the street. Anyone who wants will stop, and you will say where you want to go and then negotiate a price. It is three times as much if you speak English. The rule when I go with Boris or Ilya is to remain mute while in the car. That keeps the price at Russian standards. You never stop a car if there is more than one occupant. This way, we could get anywhere for about $3.00.

After connecting with important people, things, and locations, it was time for supper. Ilya decided he had some "things" he could fix that turned out to be what I would call Russian perogies. They were very good. But the story here focuses on Vchyslav. This guy was in love with Glenn Miller, the WWII band leader.

We had a lot of work in front of us with questions that needed to be translated, so there was much to do. Ilya didn't want Vchyslav to come since he was drunk and would waste a lot of Ilya's time. So we decided that he *would* be invited, but at the last minute, when the stuff was ready, I would ask him if I could listen to Glenn Miller shortly after dinner. I would go to his apartment for about 20 minutes, then excuse myself and get away clean, with Ilya working on the translation. That sounded like a plan!

Well, just about the time dinner was close to being ready, Vchyslav came in with a transistor radio that was tuned to a Russian station featuring Ella Fitzgerald, and he was about seven sheets to the wind. So we ate dinner with Ella blasting on the table, as he closed his eyes and moved like he was slow dancing and jabbering with Ilya in Russian. At the appointed time, I asked him if I could listen to Glenn Miller, so we went to his apartment, where we listened to about seven selections on one side of a tape. Then I excused myself on cue and went back to Ilya's with Vchyslav right on my heels. Oh well, the best-laid plans.

Red Director's Dilemmas

In 1994, Geoff Winestock, a Moscow-based correspondent for the Journal of Commerce wrote a piece that captured the essence of what it can be like to attempt an endeavor like ours in that country:

> *"Workers have not been paid for three months. No one pays their debts. It is impossible to plan ahead. Yes. you agree, the company does look to be in pretty run-down condition. But on the other hand, you know the company must be generating some cash. It does sell metal or widgets or oil to the West, it does earn hard currency from a big transport company, it does have a local monopoly.*

> *You then notice Arkady Prokopyevich, under his Soviet cut suit, is wearing a Rolex watch and an Italian tie. Inquire politely and he will tell you about his next business related trip to some sunny destination. ... He could sell off the company's property and pocket the money. But this can be risky, so the more sophisticated director will set up a related trading company that will buy the factory's goods at below cost then make an outrageous profit. ... So while the factory is doing badly, Arkady Prokopyevich is doing fine. Even though he will publicly complain about the non-payments crisis, slow bank transfers and non-payment of wages, he is secretly delighted."*

He suggested that if you are a Westerner attempting to work in a Russian company, a director like this will be difficult to work with because he will hear every proposition through the filter of how it will benefit him personally.

As we were expats in Russia at that time, it was important for us to have a heightened awareness of such potential conditions.

("Russia Parts 2-6" are found in the Notes at the end of this Chapter.)

Fun-Ditty #5.0

> *"What kind of society isn't structured on greed? The problem of social organization is how to set up an arrangement under which greed will do the least harm; capitalism is that kind of a system."*
> *- Milton Freedman*

5.1 — Russia — Training Education

There is always the need to change, grow, seek higher truths, set more aggressive objectives, and realize their fulfillment. For the Egyptian astronomer Ptolemy, the earth was the center of the universe. But Copernicus introduced profound change by placing the sun at the center. He met a great deal of resistance and persecution, but because of his theory, everything looked different.

Newton's explanation of physics was a clockwork model and is still the basis of modern engineering. But we learned from Einstein that Newton's model was partial and incomplete. His model was good enough to put a man on the moon but it couldn't explain the atom's basic structure.

Until the germ theory was developed, high percentages of women and children died during childbirth, and no one knew why. It has been said that more men died from diseases and smaller wounds than significant traumas on the front battle lines. But once the germ theory was developed, profound medical changes provided ways to understand what was happening, resulting in dramatic medical improvements and sustained life.

The need for change is nowhere more evident than in Russia, manifested during the ten-week quality course we conducted at Avto Agregat. Avto Agregat was an automotive parts manufacturer in the region of Ivanovo. I had facilitated the course many times over the previous 20 years in the United States, Asia, and other places in Russia and was always amazed at the renewal I felt taking part in those sessions. But this session was quite different.

We attacked the task on two fronts: First, technical skills (tools) necessary to compete with high quality in the global marketplace, and second, softer "teamwork" skills to help establish relationships and an environment more conducive to the successful use of these tools.

The reason for this dual attack was in part due to the difference between education and training. Training is done to improve skills, while education can change the way people think. It is not enough that workers have good skills to do their jobs. They must know *when* to use them and how to enlist the support of others to achieve even greater success than can be realized individually.

Changes continue to take place in the manufacturing world, primarily in the way that today's sophisticated customers view things. To become and remain competitive, we must continually exceed customer expectations (customer delight instead of just satisfaction). This means:

1) delivering higher quality products
2) at a lower cost
3) faster
4) with a more satisfied workforce
   (Remember good, cheap, fast, and happy?)

Many manufacturers from the west had tried sourcing products in the former Soviet Union to address one or more of these pressing requirements. In a country as vast as Russia, with a history of suffering for a greater cause, in many ways, it was like a third-world country. We had to approach the course a little differently.

We used their most important river in the country as an example, the Volga, and built a metaphor they could embrace.

This river has for centuries been the lifeblood of the Russian economy.

Our task was to view a Palace of Prosperity on the other side of the river and ask how to get across. That was the manufacturing quality problem; the palace represented high-quality products in great demand in the global marketplace. I explained that in all of our endeavors, we find differences between where we are and where we want to be, in four important ways:

1) Between actual and desired quality
2) Between actual and desired cost
3) Between how fast we get an order to the dock or a new product to the market, and the speed of our competition
4) Between a happy, optimistic, excited, motivated, innovative workforce and a crew of bedraggled, whipped, burnt-out, TGIF-hired hands

So, we defined differences as the problem, or the river, which must be crossed to bridge the difference, to get from where we are to where we need to be. The question: what is needed to cross the river?

Rivers have four relevant dimensions:

1) Width; how large is the problem, and how far are we from where we need to be?
2) Depth; how much trouble would we have if our boat sank before reaching the other side? What are the risks?

3) Speed; will we be too far downstream by the time we get to the other side to reduce the difference?
4) The nature of flow; are there hidden whirlpools to thwart our efforts or white water around the bend to create havoc and chaos? Some rivers have rock bottoms that are treacherous but predictable. Others have sand bottoms where channels shift constantly.

Each dimension must be considered before selecting the method to cross any river. Since no two rivers have the same characteristics, there is no "best skill" for all problems. We need skills (tools) to deal with each problem. Failing to understand variability is one of the industry's major problems today. The skills needed to understand and control variability were introduced during our sessions. The participants were already quite statistically literate but came away with some simple but effective technical tools.

Most problems we deal with, however, have a *personal* dimension. Something about persons or personalities usually affects a problem and its solution. Computers can do a great deal to simplify operational tasks; however, a computer cannot give praise, recognize personal grief, or act to bring adversaries to a win-win position in a heated debate. People rarely fail at a task because they don't have sufficient technical skills. Failure usually comes from the inability to work with others, to take, and to give. We found this dimension particularly relevant to our Russian audience. We addressed this important problem area with team skills covered during the sessions.

For instance, to change something, especially to remove a problem, we often have to ask someone to do something differently. People may see this as being asked to admit they have done something wrong. This was true in the Russian environment but for different reasons than we find in the west. The Russian psyche prides itself on its ability to *suffer in the pursuit of its dream.* That dream is quite individual, dependent upon personal (soft) networks as the only way to achieve the dream, to get something done.

Furthermore, in their culture, an informal personal agreement is more binding than a contract. This makes everything negotiable. The source of reluctance to admit wrongdoing lies in how it affects posturing for advantage within the network.

The big picture had to be the focus. With only the short view, people often resist change even though it might make their lives easier. The team mentality is critical here to promote a group working together for a higher purpose. When accepted, change becomes welcome, with each team member continually seeking changes to improve their job, process, and system.

A team paradigm is counter to the Russian mentality in this manner.

How did we do? Did the participants find success in these endeavors? There are few absolutes in our world. The answer is that some did, and some didn't. Many diligent participants labored through all the classes and came away with a greater understanding of technical and team skills. Others, who were caught in the "urgency of production," could not spend all the time they would have liked to and came away with less than what was possible.

One of the principles we stressed was continual improvement. Of course, we can do better next time. We hoped all participants went away with the spirit of this fact.

We can all do our jobs better and should continually seek ways to improve our work.

Fun-Ditty #5.1

> *"The only people who achieve much are those who want knowledge so badly that they seek it while the conditions are still unfavorable. Favorable conditions never come."*
>
> *– Clive S. Lewis*

5.2 – Moscow Train Incident

One Thursday night, I boarded the night train for Kineshma. The next day (Friday), we had a grand tour of the plant, reviewing the process capability with Avto Agregat personnel. This was a very impressive day.

At day's end, with a good report for Steve, we boarded the train for Moscow. 11 hours later, we were back at our home offices. We had a Quality class scheduled for later that morning. I went to my room, took a shower and gathered the materials for the lecture, then went to Ilya's to meet him and Steve before going to the class. I arrived at Ilya's at 7:30, printed my Kineshma report for Steve, and left a copy of the Fax to Mathias with a tentative schedule for the Lucas week.

I left at 8:30 to meet Arkady at the metro, but I was late. He had left earlier, so I went to class and began the lecture 15 minutes late. It was a good lecture to 9 students on Control Charts and Problem Solving.

I left the class at 12:10 and went to the metro, but I got on the train the wrong way. So after two stops, I got off and back on the right way.

I was reading a paper and missed my get-off at Rochnoi Voksal, the last metro station on the line. So, it went into the tunnel and stopped at the end. I jumped up, forced the door open, got out, and started to walk back in the dark on the track to the last exit. I was nabbed at 1:00 pm by a metro security guard, a woman in uniform, larger than I, and taken into the office in the dark of the metro tunnel.

She took my passport and started the process. Two plainclothes inspectors came, with shoulder holsters and handcuffs, who grilled me for a while. They could not communicate with me at all, so they put me in a car for a scary fast ride to the main metro office at the Aeropoint metro. That was about 3:00 pm.

I'm now sitting in the lobby, waiting for what at 4:30? No one speaks English! As I wait, I gaze at a picture in my wallet of my family and I long for them. What am I doing here??? Give me strength for one more week.

Finally, a guy shows up, another plainclothesman who could speak a little English. He and another young uniformed guy were filling out forms while asking me questions. Where was I born, who was my firm, and how did I get to the end of the tunnel?

After they filled out the forms, they went back into the office and talked to what was probably a supervisor. They argued loudly for a while, then the Sup got on the phone and talked loudly. Then they came out and asked a few more questions, wrote more, and repeated the routine with the supervisor, then two more times. It's 6 pm, and I am still here. So far, I've avoided connecting with my company in Russia or Ilya's phone number.

I got the ok to leave at 6:15, whew! I was then at Ilya's at 9:10 pm, working on the next day's class schedule for Lucas.

Fun-Ditty #5.2

> *"Education is the ability to listen to almost anything without losing your temper or your self-confidence."*
> – Robert Frost

5.3 — Statistical Quality Control

One of the key principles I needed to convey in the course is that we must understand how to obtain fair and representative samples from any production process. It isn't enough to pick the first 60 loaves that come off the assembly line during the early morning hours because this wouldn't give every loaf the same chance of being in the sample.

In experiments showing the effects of controlled factors, one must be keenly aware that results can be affected by "nuisance" factors, not controlled during the experiment. However, we don't always know what these nuisance factors are, or how they enter the experiment.

Consider an experiment comparing the impact of two training methods by exposing different groups of employees to the two methods and studying whether the type of training affects certain test scores. One must find a "fair" way to partition the workforce into two comparable groups. It would not be good to have responsible workers using one training method and the rest in the other. Such could bias the arrangement because responsible workers might score higher on tests.

This principle is important not just in manufacturing, but also in life. What if we measured our success in an endeavor, or in a relationship by too small a sample? Every worthwhile endeavor brings hardships, and every meaningful relationship has its ups and downs. So, it's important to not draw conclusions or make rash decisions based on a small number of experiences. The sampling must be wide, fair and honestly considered.

Randomized Sequencing

Randomization provides a fair way where the participants in method 1 (and method 2) are selected randomly. Randomization is essential, as we often don't know which employee characteristics could impact the comparison.

Variation in experimental results is a fact of life. It arises because of the many uncontrolled and uncontrollable factors that influence the process by replicating (repeating) the experiment, one guard against interpreting too much from the result of a single run.

Learning is an iterative process. Each time we look at the results of an experiment, we obtain further information, which allows us to focus our investigation even better.

Because of this, one should always conduct investigations in a *sequence of small experiments*. Experiments cost money, and normally one operates within a certain fixed budget. Suppose all resources are used up in one giant experiment. In that case, there is no opportunity to use the resulting knowledge and ask focused questions. Hence it is a bad idea to exhaust one's budget with a single massive experiment. It is much better to conduct a sequence of small experiments. Changing only one factor at a time is also a very poor approach, as we learned in the earlier section about Design of Experiments (DOE).

More about the importance of Randomized Sequencing can be found in the Notes for this Chapter under "Data Collection."

Fun-Ditty #5.3

> *"There are three kinds of people: those who can count and those who can't."*
>
> *- Bumper Sticker*

5.4 — Departure from Kineshma — The Painting Episode

After four years, our time was coming to an end. Following is a letter I sent to our children to close this chapter on the Russian adventure. I wrote:

> *A new vignette from the "Perils of Boris and Natasha* [our aliases]*." This fancy bit occurred last Thursday in the wind-down of Boris' activity in Kineshma at the plant called Avto Agretat.*
>
> *Yes, all good things must end, and last week was my final chapter at the village on the Volga. This has been my business home since May 1996. I had spent many weeks in Kineshma before August 1995, so you can even feel the emotion I express in announcing my departure.*

During that time, I had spent weekends in our flat in Moscow, taking the Midnight train (about 10.5 hours) Sunday nights from Moscow, then returning Thursday night from Kineshma. So, my routine was two nights on the train, two nights in Moscow, and three nights in the company hostel in Kineshma. Can't you see how this has emotionally grabbed me through these months?

The train ride at night is usually restful, with the sway of the train car and the rattle of the tracks helping lull a body to sleep. Particularly if the work schedule has been routinely filled and sleep, a rare commodity. However, during the hot summer months, the air is stifling, and tough to get much rest unless you get a rare compartment where the window will go down. The reverse is the case in the bitter winter when you pray for no air leaks and/or a functional compartment heater.

Kineshma is 400 km north of Moscow, maybe a five or six-hour car drive, but the train stops at every hamlet and village to take on and put off passengers, who take their wares to the city to sell at flea markets. Thus, the 10+ hour journey.

There are usually one or two Russian Synchroners on the train who live in Moscow and work with me in Kineshma, and we have a routine. On the ride from Kineshma to Moscow, we board the train at 6 pm. At nine, the train stops in Ivanovo, which is the major city in the Ivanovo region, of which Kineshma is a part. The stop is for one hour, right? So we lock our cabin door, walk from the train to the large train depot, walk out the front into the public square, and buy an ice cream (morozhenoe) cone, look at the scenery over, talk about the good and bad of the past week's activities, then mosey around a bit and finally 30 minutes or so back to the train, where we wait for the departure in another 20 minutes or so. The city of Ivanovo was the scene of the first Soviet in the country's history. This was the start of the activity that culminated in the 1917 revolution.

In the square is a very large black iron cast sculpture of a woman's head, with her hair blown back and up, with a very angry look on her face. This must be 20 feet high, the face on a pedestal probably 60 feet in the air. On the top of the 12-story building across the square, big letters in Russian declared Ivanovo to be the first Soviet city.

This area is the heart of Russia's textile industry. So many women textile workers during the height of Russia's glory days that the government placed a very large military base outside the city to balance nature. Today all the textile mills are shut down; it is a terribly depressed area.

So, back to my story. This Thursday, I was honored by a small meeting in our office with the Synchron team and three Avto Agregat guys who we have worked with all this time. They brought out a bottle of champagne, and each had quite a large glass. Leonid Bosloviak, my best friend in the group, asked me, "Bob, can't you break the law just once?" I thanked him but declined, drinking

Dr. Pepper with the toasts. That was about 3:30, so they wrapped that little ceremony up with a very nice hand-painted traditional Russian wooden box with a chocolate candy bar, and then they took me to the General Director's office, where Smyshlaev and a few of his deputies had me sit down to listen to more boasts and toasts (vodka this time for the Russians).

The general director, Smyshlaev, said that they are turning more and more of the responsibility for moving forward to younger people at the plant. He said that they would indeed be shipping products to the world market and that the first step was the work we had done together there. Smyshlaev then presented me with a beautiful oil painting of the village of Kineshma as viewed from the Volga River that was painted just last year by a noted Kineshma artist whose themes are only about Kineshma. He also gave me a document to allow me to take the painting out of the country when we finally leave. Big handshakes and serious heart tugs. I told them I would never remember pistons when I think about Kineshma, but I would think about the people I have shared troubles and joys with these past years, people who I consider part of my family. (actually, I will forever see pistons in my nightmares with cancer-causing ingredients in the plating)

The office team then walked with me to the hostel from the plant, where we sat together for dinner and had a third round of boasts and toasts yet, vodka no less, me with my soft drink. They *each said good and flattering things. I told them I wished my mother could have heard what they all said, that she would have believed them. It was a heart-tugging time; these are really a good bunch to work with. They often don't respond in traditionally expected ways, taking longer to do things with different priorities and expectations, but time must be an important ally in making this transformation. It is clear that they've just read from a different book than we have.*

The office team got us all in two cars for the trip to the train station (vokzal), where they found a guy with a camera who took pictures of the group. Then Victor Shishkin and I departed for our routine trip to Moscow at 6 pm. I had my clothes and stuff, computer, scanner, zip, printer, plus a bunch of paraphernalia that had accumulated through the months. Additionally, I had this beautiful oil painting as my remembrance gift from the Avto Agregat plant. And away we went.

So, on schedule, we stopped in Ivanovo at 9 pm. After our first morozhenoe, we had wasted fifteen minutes, so we had another and took a slow walk around the angry lady. At the 40-minute point, we slowly walked through the train station to stand on the platform where..., there was no train! Oh, my! No clothes and stuff, computer, scanner, zip, printer, paraphernalia, or picture. Gone. I looked at Victor; he looked at me, then he ran to the office in the station to find out what had happened! It seems that on this day, this very day, they changed the train schedule for only a 20-minute stop, not the one-hour old.

He explained the situation; they got on the phone to call Moscow and alert him of the difficulty. It turned out we weren't the only ones caught in the bind. The train arranged for a bus going to Moscow to be routed by the station, and several of us took empty seats and started the long journey by about 11 pm. It was very crowded, completely full after we got on. The seats reclined, but you couldn't sit straight if the person in front had his seat reclined, so they were all tightly reclined. They had a fairly large TV screen at the front of the bus, which had Russian music videos on pretty loudly. A couple of guys were smoking two seats in front of us. This was not a lot of fun. All this time, I'm thinking, "I'll never see any of my things again."

We arrived at a different train station in Moscow than where we were to have arrived on our train. It was about 5 am, and the train wasn't supposed to arrive until 5:30, so we thought we might be able to get there when it arrived to get on and get our stuff before it drifted off into oblivion. We caught a taxi where we got off the bus, got us as close as possible to the train station, then ran as fast as possible to the platform where the train was to have arrived.

And there it was, with people just starting to get off. Viola! We ran to the very end, but there was no car number 6??? Well, the train we were on arrived 30 minutes ago since it didn't wait so long in Ivanovo. This was a different train.

Suspicions confirmed. We would never see our stuff.

Victor made his way to the train security police officers, up to three flights of stairs, down a very long corridor, then down three flights of stairs to the office. It was filled with important-looking guys in uniforms.

After heavy dialog, Victor was let into a closet where low and behold, there were all of our bags, everything except the picture. They said it was in another train station, where the train went after its earlier arrival.

They said we would have to wait a while, but it would be brought to us.

Alexei, our driver, had arrived to pick me up, and he assessed the situation. We would wait, and Victor could go on to his home. Alexei said, "Bob, this is very bad, waiting. You won't see your picture again."

We waited, nonetheless, for almost two hours. Alexei said the shift of security police changed at 8 am, and if we hadn't gotten the picture by then, it was a dead issue. But just before eight, a young man in uniform came down the street with the picture and a grin. I tried to pay him 100,000 rubles ($20.00) as a reward, but he refused with a grin and went on his way.

Alexei said, "Bob, this has been a very good day for both of us. For you, because you got all your *things back, for me because I know that all things in Russia are not bad."*

Amen to that. I am now looking forward to my next assignment.

Fun-Ditty #5.4

"Years may wrinkle the skin, but to give up enthusiasm wrinkles the soul.... Worry, fear, and self-distrust bow the heart and turns the spirit back to dust. Whether sixty or sixteen, there is in every human being's heart the lure of wonder, the unfailing child-like appetite for what's next, and the joy of the game of living. ...[A]s long as your aerials are up, to catch the waves of optimism, there is hope you may die young at eighty."

– Samual Ullman

NOTES ON CHAPTER 5

Additional thoughts related to this chapter:

Russia Part 2

2/22/94 This piece was from St. Petersburg, now dividing my time between St. Petersburg and Moscow. Missed the bus again this morning. I got to bed last night at 10:30, thought I had the jet lag licked, but woke up at 2 am as though it was the middle of the day. So I flipped the TV on, watched Tom Brokaw do the evening news, then watched the last half of a Robert Taylor black and white movie. I don't know when I finally got to sleep. Anyway, the desk didn't give me a wake-up call. The second time, I'd better get an alarm clock.

Ed Frey talked to me about how I could contribute half time to a very sorry operation. His biggest problem, or the one he doesn't have covered well, was with marketing. He explained it and felt like I could manage it half-time. So, I'm a marketing guru, helping an inept Russian try to get the department turned around. It's not really marketing but sales. It is not difficult to see where the problems are.

The difficulty is getting people who have done what they were told for all their professional careers to think. Suddenly, the old Russian market they have served all these years is not doing so well, so orders are down, and the factor is underutilized. It's a new thought to try to go out and try to sell their product. They are suspicious of any expat (non-Russian) customer. The key is to get performance measures so they can become accountable for their jobs.

When they did the first sales forecast, the numbers were what the plant could produce, not what they expected to sell. I've been working on that concept for the last three days. And it goes with less than half-speed with the translators. But I felt like a few lights went on today. Some group members have the attitude, "we outlived the Germans 200 years; we'll outlast Booz-Allen too." However, it will probably never change for them.

I will work the Booz tomorrow and Thursday, then work with two potential Xerox printer manufacturers with Boris on Friday. We will take a train Friday night to Moscow (a Pullman type with separate compartments) and begin the Synchron Q training on Saturday. We will return to St. Petersburg on Tuesday. I will be able to look for a branch in Moscow Sunday. When I get back, I'm going to look for an apartment for us in earnest. The ones I have seen are ones the Booz guys have been looking at. I don't like the area they are in. You will be able to go to Moscow with me when I go during this train-the-trainer startup schedule. The Booz 5 on, one off would let us spend a week in Europe or wherever or fly on to the states. The Booz laptop computer went out on me. My brain is in the beastly thing. Hope I can get it fixed.

Russia Part 3

What a great talk we had last night. I just finished breakfast, then walked around the ship on the open deck. It's 8:30, only a little light. The days are short here. There are several people already out on the ice fishing. The fish they catch are only about 3 to 6 inches long, like sardines. But one guy had a small bag filled with them. The people on the ice are really friendly even though we can't communicate.

As Boris and I were walking from the Trade show to the hotel, a funny-looking vehicle came across the ice near the bank. A guy climbed out the top and hollered in Russian. Boris talked with him for a while, then Boris invited me to take a ride on the thing, which cost $5.00. The guy was a little scraggly type, about 60, and his vehicle had a big propeller in the air, and it would cruise about 40 mph just off the ice surface. It was a hoot. That was when we stopped and spoke to some of the ice fishermen. The guy had pictures of his trips to the waters (ice) above Siberia and the big mammoth tusks they had found.

I'm waiting for Boris. He will come at 9:00, so we can organize what we learned at the trade show for Steve and Ilya. They will be here at 10:00. Looking forward to this day.

The computer quit on me, and I don't know what's wrong. Hope I can get it going when I get back to work tomorrow. There is a business center here on the ship, and they have computers for rent, so I'm not totally shut down. Well, hon, I need to get this package ready for the mail. Much love, Bob

2/23/94 I'm sitting here en route to Helsinki, Finland, on Finnair Airlines. It's 8:40 am, and I just finished the meal served. It was very good, rice and chicken. The trip to the airport (Cleveland) was quick. The cabbie was a bit unkempt, with scraggly long hair and a beard, smoked all the way but not a bad sort. He and his brother had lived in one of the units at Trenton when they were new, over 20 years ago or so, he said.

The TWA 3:30 flight I was scheduled for had been canceled. That is why Sue got me on an earlier flight on Delta. That was good since I had to take the bus to the Finnair terminal from Delta when I got to Kennedy. I forgot how big a real international airport could be. Anyway, I didn't have a minute to spare.

Ed brought me the printer just at boarding time. We didn't have much time to talk. He won't come to St. Petersburg for two weeks. He just made a new hot contact with a guy who wants to buy rope from Russia. I need to get Ilya looking for samples right away. While I was with Maurice this morning, he was on the phone with Richard in Paris, with more (different) diamond deals going on. I will spend about half my time managing the three guys on the Stumhammer job (2 Russia and one a retired foundry expert) and half time working Synchron deals. One of the hottest things right now is Synchron University. They are working with a guy who is starting a technical/engineering school at two locations and wants to do it with us. He will give us an entire floor in a big Booz-Allen-type building. I'll keep you updated. Sounds like many good opportunities are coming from several angles.

They have located a company that can build the Xerox printer and wants it badly. That is something that will make my initial job much easier. They have a map on the TV monitor showing where the plane is on the route and words telling how much farther to go, how many hours more, our altitude, and speed. We have 2957 more miles, 5 ½ hours more. Everyone on the plane is reading and speaking in Finnish!

I just caught a lot of the Olympic skating and saw Kerrigan do very well. It looked lit. Tonja was in 11th place. Too bad. I've been spending all my time at Booz trying to get a handle on it.

2/25/94 It was so good talking to you twice on the phone last night. I just had breakfast with Boris and Jim and getting ready to visit a couple of plants with Ilya and Boris. Jim is the Booz guy who is from Dallas. We ride to work together in the van each day. He was married in the same year we were. Tonight Ilya and I will ride to Moscow on the train to return Tuesday. Steve and Maurice should be here when we return.

Interestingly, the elevators are shut down at 6:30 pm in the plan to save energy costs. We have to walk down from the 7th floor whenever we work after that. Good thing it's down and not up. Small blessings. Got to go. Love you, Bob.

Russia Part 4 – Trip Report, Bob Robertson, St. Petersburg, Russia, April 22 – 30 Saturday, April 30, 1994

"I'll summarize the past week and a half in St. Petersburg since my return on Friday, April 22, from the comforts of this Delta Flight 25. I can't express the profound relief felt being on the plane in my seat, knowing the luggage is checked through and that several hours lie ahead without a line to wait in. It began when the driver picked me up at the hotel at 6:05 am, getting to the airport at 6:50. I had three very heavy pieces of luggage to check through. I was weighed down by the many books and manuals I had for the classes in Moscow.

The first stop was the customs desk, where all the luggage goes through the x-ray, and they check our declarations. The biggest thing they check for is to see that you are not taking more dollars or rubles out of the country than you brought in. They will just summarily pluck any difference from your person. That is, they don't want you taking wealth out of the country, only bringing it in. They are also cautious about antique paintings or drawings. Specific rules about how old such a piece is and how much it is worth determine whether you can take it out. One party at the hotel told me they have a routine to smuggle anything into Finland that doesn't meet the requirements. They made a deal with the widow of a famous painter in St. Petersburg and are surreptitiously removing all of the works in the collection.

The last time I went through this routine, I was behind a party with Israeli passports, and customs went through every bag enthusiastically, albeit during a very long wait. They have never questioned my declarations (must be the honest face???...)

Anyway, I spent about 20 minutes in that line with the stack of luggage (I also had three pieces of carry-on luggage, a briefcase, a computer, and a shaving kit). The next line was the airline check-in. My ticket said the flight was to depart at 7:40, but the sign behind the counter said 7:00. It was 7:15 when I saw that. But not to worry, I was in a line behind about 20 people on the same flight, so I figured they would make allowances. Upon finally getting to the counter, jockeying my six pieces, it was 7:40, they didn't argue with the third piece to check through, and I was finally unburdened with the biggies.

The next line was the passport booth, only another 15 minutes, and I found myself at the door behind which everyone on the flight was waiting for a bus to take us out to the flight. I was the last to squeeze onto the bus as the doors slammed shut, and away we went. The plane was not close to the air terminal. As I fell off when the doors opened, it put me at the front of the line, and I was the first onto the plane. I could put my carry-on stuff anywhere. So I did. And here I am, reflecting on the events of the past ten days with my fingers at the keyboard.

"The events began when I left Cleveland at 2:30 on Thursday the 21st, arrived at Kennedy at 4:00, then left for Stockholm at 6:45, then arrived in St. Petersburg at 1:30 Friday afternoon. I spent about 4 hours at the plant that afternoon before going to the hotel. Cleaned off my desk and got an update from Ed for the following week. The board meeting was scheduled for Tuesday, so we had Monday to pull the deck together for their presentation. We had all been working toward this, so there was no panic. We left for the hotel at about 7:00.

"As I went into the hotel, I met Ilya, Ed, and Boris coming out. Ilya and Ed took the train to Moscow that evening, and Boris was going the next day. I was also scheduled to take the midnight train for Saturday classes. Anyway, we had time to talk about the situation before they left. Since I was going on a later train that same night, Boris stayed in my room at the hotel.

Ilya met me on the train with Ed and took me to the first session at MAMI (Institute in Moscow), where we discussed things with the 20 participants. The materials weren't fully translated for this session, so we scheduled the first class next time and just answered questions about Synchron.

A woman, Ludmila Konareva (Ph.D., author, lecturer on TQM, etc., etc.), came under the invitation of Vchyslav (Ilya's KGB neighbor). She wanted to find out what it was all about. Ilya said a few opening comments, then left after asking her to translate for me. It was a good move as she also agreed to translate for the afternoon session in Zelenograd. The first group (Quality Auditing) mostly wanted to know what Synchron was offering down the road. She particularly wanted to know who would fund this effort and where the money was coming from.

I told them the effort would be self-funding with the partnerships established between Russian and Western companies. It wasn't in place yet, and this effort is offered as a community service as a precursor to the big things coming. Our model is to establish qualified people in the Quality disciplines through networking, education, and certification through Synchron. Hence, people are ready when the need arises. There are no promises, and everybody who takes and passes the class or even becomes officially "Synchron certified" won't get a job or make any money. Some of those in the pool will be tapped when the needs are established. Konareva was most concerned about this aspect but felt ok by the day's end.

"Ed attended the session, and afterward, Ilya discussed heavy matters with attendees. Ed had hoped to be able to spend some time with me discussing critical issues and frustrations, but Ilya had the time tightly blocked. Since time was running short and Ilya was hard to slow down when promoting his dreams, Ed, Konareva, and I slipped out and lined a ride up to Zelenograd for the afternoon session without talking to Ilya. This turned out to be a good move. We could talk about it out of earshot of anyone else involved during breaks and after the session. Ilya hadn't told Ed we were having a partner meeting in Cleveland the first week in May. All Russian companies are closed that week for the national May-Day holiday. Ilya had told Ed he should stay and work on his Russian. I told Ed he had to talk to Steve and to be there.

"The afternoon session went as scheduled. The translation was complete except for the problems section. That wasn't too cool, but it is more apparent how difficult it is to do the translation task. Ludmila said during the afternoon session that much of the translation was wrong. I cautioned her not to badmouth the free help we were getting, and she mellowed out and volunteered to help in the future.

"The three of us had dinner at a Georgian (Russian cuisine) restaurant in Moscow, then went to the train at 11:00 pm, and then returned to St. Petersburg. Back to the perils of ZTL.

The board meeting had been scheduled for Tuesday. This was the day they would decide if Booz would continue beyond this week. It had been assumed they would extend, but it wasn't clear what conditions would accompany the extension.

When I got to the hotel at about 9:00 Sunday morning, a note asked me to call Ed. They had moved the board meeting to Monday, and we needed a team meeting at noon on Sunday to pull it together. We worked until early evening and with still a lot of work to complete Monday morning.

I had a good marketing meeting with Makarov on Monday, reviewed the fax he sent me last week while I was in the states, and agreed on the new marketing organization format. This was necessary for the presentation to be given to the board. The board didn't complete their work on Monday, so it was pushed out to Tuesday. Work continued tweaking the deck. We didn't know the actual result until Wednesday morning. They didn't extend.

The storyline was they were happy with Booz's performance, but they were out of money. They wanted to raise some cash and bring us back in one to three months.

Monday and Tuesday had been panic days working on the deck for the board meeting, then when word came of no extension. The new story was to put another deck together as a lever so we could say, "this is what you must do to keep it going without us." The intent was double-edged; 1st, we wanted them to fail so they would see how badly they needed us, and 2nd, to provide enough valid help so they would succeed. Figure that out! So back to the computers, printers, and copiers.

We worked until 11:00 Wednesday night and 10:30 Thursday night. Tempers were hot, the air was blue with foul, abusive language, and nothing seemed to work. The main printer went on the fritz. Dennis took the power adapters for the computers with him (he left Wednesday afternoon), so we couldn't use the other printer and the computer simultaneously. That meant the one computer that could print on that particular printer could only work on battery power while the printer was working. Of course, that required stopping after several printed pages to move the power back to the computer while its battery was recharged.

Both decks had to be done in Russian and English. We had six translators, and Yuri and Viktor helped do the Russian version as the four of us (Ed, Jim, Pete, and Dennis before he left) did our English version. Of course, we made changes continually that required going back to the translator's Russian version.

All were trying to get on the computer/printer combination. We had other computers to do our work but had to copy the stuff on a disk and print from the only computer with that printer driver. Tempers were frayed. Viktor gave a handwritten version of his work and wasn't happy with the computer version one of the translators printed. He said something in his broken English that the translator and one of the Booz managers took as an insult, and we almost had a fistfight. It was cleared up the next day after the heat of the battle cooled.

Jim Furey was the Booz project manager-elect with Ed's departure and was taking responsibility for both decks. He has been through some tough times since coming to St. Pete in February, about the same time I did. He had his camera stolen about the first week. His room was broken into at the hotel, and he lost a bunch of money and important papers a couple of weeks later. He fell and broke his arm, which had been in a cast for the past six weeks, and then had his briefcase stolen out of his office at the factory last week, losing his passport, visa, and more money along with a bunch of traveler's checks (which he got replaced). He is also a diabetic and has to take insulin shots four times a day. Then to top it all off, he got the bug and has felt totally drained the past week with fevers, chills, and total exhaustion. With this wrap-up Chinese fire drill, Jim was not a happy camper. With him screaming for the work to get done, none of us were happy campers either.

I talked to Maurice Thursday morning and discussed the upcoming meetings in Cleveland. He felt like I needed to move the Moscow classes out a week so I would be able to attend each day next week. I left word on Ilya's machine of the push-out, asking him to notify all the participants. Then I called Rubanik's secretary in Zelenograd and asked her to notify everyone. Then I called Ludmila and asked her the same. They told me it would be taken care of, so the next sessions are scheduled for May 14.

Friday arrived. We were scheduled to meet at noon to present the go-forward plan to Chernychev (head guy, plant manager) and seven of his directors. The meeting was held in a big conference room on the 7th floor. It had one long table around which sat the eight Russian managers, six Booz guys, including Yuri and Viktor, and four interpreters. It has large double-plate glass windows across one wall that hasn't been washed in years. The view is a drab picture of many other factories like theirs, tall smokestacks with no color at all this time of year. The chairs are wooden, straight-backed with faded upholstery above the table line where the sun's rays had shone. All the rooms in this office building have 12 ft. ceilings, and the windows in this room are over eight feet high.

Chernychev kicked the meeting off on a good note, saying this should be an open exchange of ideas for their benefit. Ed turned the presentation over to Jim, who went through the first part, which lasted until 2:30. He had Yuri and Pete go through their sections with an overhead projector with each page of the deck. Ed gave only Chernychev a Russian copy at the start of the meeting. He didn't give the others a Russian copy until the end of the meeting. Chernychev is a colorful character. It seems his hair is always disheveled (morning hair), with the top button of his shirt undone and his tie loose. He becomes very animated when discussing issues, particularly when he is not happy with one of his directors.

The meeting seemed to go without controversy, and the Russians accepted the presentation quite well. It was a fascinating scene, however, as I listened to the din of the session. There were eight Russians, Ed, Jim, Pete and I, each with our interpreters, and Yuri and Viktor. So, as a Russian was speaking, four other conversations were going on with our interpreters telling us what the Russian was saying. When another Russian would pick up on the conversation, and they would start tossing an issue back and forth, it wasn't clear which Russian our interpreters were speaking. Occasionally, I would get more interested in what Ed's interpreter was saying than mine. That was the "din…."

The meeting broke at 2:15 for 20 minutes. I went downstairs for a bowl of soup. We had lunch each day on the ground floor, a nice setting in a room served by a gentlewoman who would bring us each course and provide a small salad, soup, then the main dish. She is an ex-engineer at the plant but is happy to have a job providing this service. It was a seven-floor elevator ride when the elevator was working.

They turn it off at the end of the first shift to conserve energy which means we always walk down at the end of the day and up when activity takes us out in the late afternoon. The plant is generally quite dark as a further measure to reduce energy costs. The halls are quite dark, and most rooms get their light from the large windows. I don't know if that has anything to do with the drinking problem at the plant. They tell me half the casting complex is usually tanked. Not as bad in the Stamping/Forging complex, but still pretty severe.

Russia Part 5 – Follow-up

Wednesday, 3/22/95 – Steve returned to the states. I spent the day visiting the ZIL plant in Mtensk and received what sounded like an emergency call from my wife. Steve had called from Ilya's with a note to call home. I got hold of Arkady, who reported someone had stolen my cash card and was charging a lot of stuff, that I should call my wife.

I decided to call her Thursday morning from Ilya's since it was about 3 am where she was. We boarded the train at 10:00 pm for the return.

Thursday, 3/23/95 – Arrived at Moscow train station at 6:30 am. I went to Ilya's for a report and Got Ilya out of bed at about 7 am. I stressed that I had to call my wife due to an emergency. He asked if I had to do it now. I said yes, and he grumbled. He grumbled because there was a blond head of hair peeking out from under the sheets of his bed (the phone was in his bedroom). I went ahead and called my wife and got that worked out without a stir from the sweet young thing in the bed.

Friday, 3/24/95 – Arkady came at 9 am and worked with me translating Geller's report on the ZIL casting plant. I polished up the Synchron Q business plan and tried to fax it to Steve all day, finally faxing it to Maurice at the day's end since Steve's fax wasn't picking up. Arkady left at 7 pm. I lockup up at 10 pm and took a cab to the Leningradsky train station (Vokzal), where I boarded with Mathius. We talked shop until about 12:30 pm.

Saturday 3/25/95 – Arrived in St. Petersburg at 8:20 am, where the Naviins driver met us and whisked Neil Mathius and me to the Naviins' office. Leonid was there, the lecture was scheduled to begin at 9:30, and they had snacks for us. The management wanted Mathius to go to their hotel and meet back for the start of the meeting after the lecture, but Neil wanted to take part in the lecture. So while they enjoyed the snacks, I went to the lecture room to try to set up the overhead projector. Two lamps burned out while trying to set it up, so I had to do without them. I started at 9:30, lectured until 10:40 and finished what I wanted to cover then took a break. After the break, Mathius spoke for about 20 minutes about the importance of quality to Lucas. It turned out to be a pretty good day. Mathius, seeing firsthand what we are doing with the quality classes, can now give an accurate report.

I think Ilya was a little drunk at this time, not offensively so but feeling no pain. He told me later how the pressure has been so great on him with Benz canceling his visit and Mathius here to see the new status that he came within an inch of canceling the whole thing. The Naviins guys made a presentation for about an hour with charts and visual aids while Leonid translated. Ilya was upset that Leonid hadn't practiced the translation and that it didn't come across as smoother.

Monday, 3/27/95 – The landscape hasn't changed much. A lot of what looks like quakies and pines are on the way. We got to Bugulma at 11:30, meaning we were on the train for 26 hours. Mr. Naumov met us on the train with a bus that took us to Almetevsk, about 30 minutes away. We had lunch and then a three-hour plant tour. After the tour of what is a good possibility for a long-term relationship, we went to the GD's office and talked for over an hour. He speaks a little English, a very poised professional, probably in his late 40s or early 50s. He immediately understood the Synchron concept and, jokingly, said, "Let's go!"

Realizing there is much to talk about before we "go," we made tentative plans to further the discussion later. He said he wasn't sure a Joint Venture would be the best vehicle for a cooperative relationship. We agreed and said much discussion lies ahead before we agree on those details. I told him that whatever arrangement we finally came up with still boiled down to mutual trust between us. I hoped we could develop that kind of mutual trust. He said he agreed with that and was happy to hear our priorities were in the right place. It was an open and easy meeting, having dinner at the end with many vodka toasts.

This region is partly Muslim. The chief metallurgist who met us on the train told us about 40% of the 3000 workers at the plant are Tatars (the region is Tatarskstan), with the balance of various Russians. The GD had his son with him at the dinner meeting. A young strapping guy of about 18 looked a lot like my son. I made my usual toast to the families of us all who make this all worthwhile. How grateful I was the son (Ivan) was there.

I'm never sure how this toast goes over. As I looked around the table, over half the men may not have been married. At one point, I told the GD what a great favor the Russians did by sending up the first Sputnik with Yuri Gagarin. I was a young engineer in the aerospace industry, and that event scared us all in America. The US Government coffers opened up, and we could spend money without common sense or reason, which helped put us on the moon. He said the same thing happened when he was in the aerospace industry in Russia when a Soviet pilot flew a

MIG-25 to Japan, giving the US all their secret technology. They were also scared, with a further turn of the economic funds available to the Russians.

Tuesday 3/28/95 This experience, with positive vibes about what might become long-term cooperation between the East and the West, makes me feel I'm where I should be. At about noon, the five of us got to the train station in Bugulma, where we bought tickets that weren't reserved. It just meant we took what wasn't occupied when we got on. However, Geller and Kolesnikov had it aced, and we got a full four-bunk compartment together. It always amazes me how they come up with what turns out to be a good meal from pockets and sacks and how sophisticated they do it. There were five of us sitting on the two cots sharing bread sliced from a whole loaf with canned salmon and sliced sausages along with cucumbers Geller sliced with his Swiss knife. They had coffee and tea while I had an orange drink they acquired somewhere, then cakes (quite large cookies) enough for all.

At about 7 in the evening, we went through the town of Ulyanovsk, which is the native home of Lenin. We passed a hill upon which a beautiful white building was well-lit, which looked like the Arizona temple, a memorial for Lenin built near his parents' home.

Wednesday, 3/29/95 – Stopped for a 20-minute passenger pickup in a little town at 8 am. Several old ladies (babushkas) came through the train selling bread, sausages, drinks, etc. All sausage here is called "kielbasa," whether it is pepperoni, salami, or any other variation. All kielbasa. I stopped at Rosievska at about 12:30 for 15 minutes. I found a kiosk near the train station where I bought a Snickers, savored it over the next 10 minutes, and arrived in Moscow at 5:00 pm.

Thursday, 3/30/95 – Ilya went over his plan for the training, saying we had to do it all on weekends since the Institute where he scheduled the classes might throw us out of the room. So we changed the schedule to all four weeks being Friday, Saturday, and Sunday. He also told me in big technicolor terms what a great deal he got with the Institute, only $100 for three days. He really put them down, and they wanted twice that, but he told them where to go and got the original deal he offered! How could this have ever worked at all without his infinite skills????

Friday, 3/31/95 – Started the first day of training. Ilya didn't arrive until after 2 pm. Nobody knew what to do at 9:30 when it was supposed to start. Adler more or less took over, and Arkady spent the morning going over DOS and Lexicon on the PCs until Ilya arrived. The classes were scheduled at NATI this week. This is the Institute where we had the final few classes in Quality Auditing. Ilya started rambling with no agenda, no goal, or nothing special he wanted to cover. I was boiling, Garshkov complained during the first break. Arkady thought it was a colossal waste of time. At one point, Ilya asked if I thought what he had proposed was ok. It had to do with finding who was at fault for things not getting done as planned.

I said we needed to quit trying to place blame and get down to training the people in what we expect them to do! He picked up on that, saying that was exactly what he wanted me to say, then rambled in another direction for a couple of hours. At the end of the day, Ilya got Adler with me to discuss what should take place the next day. I said he had to devise an agenda that at least listed what he wanted to cover or accomplish. He said, "let me and Adler come up with a plan and we'll tell you, ok?" Ok. After five minutes, they said they would do more of Ilya's stuff in the morning and then work on computers with Arkady in the afternoon.

Saturday, 4/1/95 – We waited for Ilya. We were supposed to start at 9:30 am. I bet Leonid that Ilya wouldn't arrive before 10:00. He came at 9:58, and I owed Leonid a coke. I prepared a complete agenda for the four weeks of scheduled training, including the days and times of each training session. Ilya had suggested we meet only on weekends to get the room at a lower rent and not be put out due to some director's meeting during the week. I told him I decided the weekends were unacceptable and that I wouldn't ask the team to give up four weekends when it wasn't necessary. Therefore, the training schedule I gave everyone had no Sundays and only one Saturday. I handed this to everyone before Ilya arrived.

He began rambling, which continued through the day. He had no agenda on paper or in his head. I typed as fast as possible as different translators took turns telling me what Ilya was telling them. It was my distinct impression that Ilya had been drinking, but only an impression. On several occasions, I would stop Ilya and ask him to clarify what he had just said, was what I heard really what he meant?

He would sidestep the questions and make a joke of it. I gave up and just tried to capture his message. After the lunch break, he didn't do the computer bit. He kept rambling on about some article he had read the night before about a management style. It was quite obvious he was killing time without any objective. Arkady, who is no longer on the payroll but had come in for the day to facilitate the computer training after lunch, was a bit distressed. Ilya asked him at about 4:00 if he had a problem and asked him to leave. On his way out, Arkady told Ilya in front of the group that Ilya was assassinating the entire staff with his lectures.

I had to pick this much up from bits and pieces from participants later. Later Ilya told me about what an ingrate Arkady is and how much grief he had brought on the group. Ilya told me what Arkady had said and that he (Ilya) asked the group if they felt like they were being assassinated? And nobody said "yes!" So, see what a turkey Arkady is? After the lecture, I got Ilya aside and sat down with him for 20 minutes, telling him how badly I thought the training was going. I reminded him that he said at one point on the first day that if anyone on the team saw us going in the wrong direction and didn't say something, we were wrong. I said, "Ilya, we're going in the wrong direction."

I reiterated my stance on the importance of an agenda and some structure in what we did. I had him read the article I have carried around, "Why smart people do dumb things." I suggested that one of the problems brilliant people have is the impression they don't need any structure. I told him we were trying to be professional and that one of the most unprofessional things is to go before a group so unprepared. I said that our task is to be leaders, but if we go at it this way, nobody will want to follow us. Then he told me how difficult it is to do everything yourself when you don't even have time to get a good night's sleep and have to be up until 2 am preparing for the lecture. Who has time to think of an agenda? Don't I think he doesn't want to do it right, with an agenda and all? Whew.

Sunday 4/2/95 – More of the same, random rambling. I left at 11:00 to go to church and returned at 4:00. It was as if I hadn't left. He had rescheduled all the training classes for Friday, Saturday, and Sunday. He said the team members had insisted that they couldn't get their work done during the week if they spent all their time in class. I asked myself, is any of this worth it?

Monday 4/3/95 – I went to the Hotel Metropole business center, where I called the companies on the Joint Venture list we had mailed to last June. Confirmed the companies that were still operating and had current fax numbers. I then worked on the Synchron Q fax letter to sell the product, then got to the Mezdunarodnya Hotel, where I got three letters faxed.

Friday, 4/7/95 – We held the training class, starting with the Desert Survival exercise. It went well and lasted until the 12:30 lunch brake. We all ate at the plant cafeteria, and then Rubanik did the afternoon. It went very well. He had an assistant there to videotape the day's proceedings. I went to Ilya's at 8:30 pm and called and told my wife I had decided not to return, faxed the certification exam stuff to ASQC, called Steve and told him I didn't want to return to Russia. He was very supportive and understood that it wasn't what I had wanted, to be away from my family like this. He asked if I could meet with him in Florida the week after I was in Utah. He suggested when quality issues come up, maybe I can spend a week in Russia once in a while.

Saturday, 4/8/95 – I couldn't get out of bed; my back was killing me. Leonid came to get me to go to class, I begged off and said to tell Rubanik to take over, and I will be there after lunch. I got to the class at 1:30, and they were getting ready to do a lunch break. Yuri Adler was there helping Rubanik do his bit on Deming. It seemed to go pretty well. I hadn't been able to put many ideas together, so I introduced to them the concept of variation by having them do the Beads-1 computer simulation, where they tried to optimize the Beads production process.

Class ended just after 5 pm. It went well, I was in a lot of pain, but the pain pills I got at Ilya's were doing a fairly good job. Rubanik gave me a ride back to the Gastinitsa after class. I tried to rest, but it wasn't easy. I called Serge Bushman (Elders quorum president) at 8:30 and asked him if he could come and give me a blessing. He said sure. It was just after 10:30 when he and Pres. Atkins (Branch President) arrived and gave me a blessing. It was a choice. I waited outside for them, giving them only an address on the street (28 Chesovaya). I figured it would take them over a half hour to arrive. I got the number from the desk clerk but realized when I was outside waiting for them that it was 23, not 28. They took the metro and then walked, looking for the place. I was so happy to see them. This is such a great gospel! I had my first full night's sleep in a long time.

Sunday, 4/9/95 – I got to class on time. I listened to Rubanik do his "cooperation game" that he got from the British Deming Association. It was an excellent setup where four teams tried to make choices to maximize their profits. It was set in a clever way where the only way to maximize profits was to cooperate. Dr. Adler spoke about process capability and the choice of sample size. Rubanik turned it over to me at 11:30. Everyone asked, "can we take a break?" I said no since we would be finished in about 30 minutes.

I took the time to punch up the value of Rubanik's cooperation game and related it to our trying to establish cooperative agreements between Western and Russian companies. I further spoke about the advantage of competition for getting the most out of the workforce in the spirit of teamwork, then about what Deming spoke of as the balance between these two ideas; cooperation and competition.

I finished with the counsel of Juran in getting things right with the workforce that three things are essential from the management position so that they have fully empowered the workforce: 1) a clear written statement of what is expected of the employee, 2) a clear understanding of how each employee is doing against those expectations, and 3) the ability the change any difference between 1 and 2. I told them they had to insist on these three things from an employer to make their maximum contribution.

Lastly, I told them to go home and enjoy their families, smell the roses, coffee, or whatever is good. Rubanik gave me a ride home. It is now Sunday evening. I will turn this computer over to Geller before he goes to St. Petersburg tonight and picks up my other one in Cleveland being repaired. So this is my swan song for now. I'm out of here!!!!

The return flight stopped first in Warsaw, Poland, Frankfurt, Germany, London, and then to Cincinnati. A short jump from there to home. I thought of the haunting refrain of Jo Stafford from the '50s, "Far away places, with strange-sounding names… are calling me, calling me…." Considering these last two weeks. Who would have thought?

Russia Part 6 – On-going Efforts

Last night (Wednesday), we had a hot dinner, the same group, and quite a lot of beer and vodka. The discussion continued until 9:30, with Jim spouting theories and procedures he felt were important. Jim's background is Industrial Engineering, with many years working for Booz-Allen. He started as a journeyman machinist and went to school nights at Lasalle University in Philadelphia. He lived in Texas for many years, was an avid hunter and fisherman then moved to the Cleveland area a few years ago. He has four grown children, two boys and two girls. He is only six months younger than me, and we have a lot in common.

On the other hand, he is very foul-mouthed and has an alcohol problem. He has diabetes and has to give himself shots at least three times a day. He also has high blood pressure. He is not in very good condition. He is separated from his wife and now lives with a young Russian gal in St. Petersburg. She was a translator for Booz on the LZTL job in St. Petersburg just over three years ago. Jim was on that job then also where he met Alicia.

During last night's discussion, Jim said we talk too much in Russia and that he is tired of meetings and blah-blah-blah. And the night droned on as Jim kept talking and talking. Novikov said that we had meetings on Fridays in the past where we learned a lot from each other and that it was valuable time referring specifically to the classes I taught. He felt like we needed to keep doing some of that. He referred to the Covey Important-Urgent matrix and Q1, Q2, Q3, and Q4. He said we were sharpening our saws in the Friday meetings in Q2.

Jim asked, in all the time you spent in those meetings or classes, what did you ever learn that was worth anything you used on the job? He pointedly asked Khabi, what three things did you learn from Bob's classes that you have used on the job? Khabi said it was important that he still used teamwork, the ability to understand how we are a team and that we don't argue or fight among ourselves. The second thing was the auditing classes, how to conduct a quality audit and what to look for in the factories where we work. The third thing was how to deal with Russians to get them to a western mentality in manufacturing operations. Novikov agreed with Khabi the whole time. Jim wasn't convinced, saying we needed to talk less and do more. And then he talked for another hour.

Thursday, May 23, 1996 - This morning, we had breakfast in the hostel at 8 am, Jim Furey, Leonid Bosloviak, Dr. Novikov, Dr. Khabi, Vladimir Zaitsev, Oleg Zupnik, and I. Bliney, which is pancakes, small salad, juice, black bread (chorny Xleb), and much butter. The guys had very black coffee. On the pancakes, we put butter, then a condensed milk-sugar mix that serves as syrup, pretty good. I will try to catch up today since I have some coast time. I'm here on a one-month trial basis. When I was laid off at Manco, Maurice and I decided to try Synchron again for a one-month trial. I'm now sitting in the Synchron office typing away while Jim is working on a fax, and the Russians are talking a mile a minute, making plans for the day.

Jim has taken a very positive attitude towards me, I think because we hit it off talking about hunting and fishing. I told him on the walk to the hostel yesterday at the end of the day that, to clarify, I was only on a one-month trial. I told him some of the reasons I left eight months ago, particularly that I felt like I got no support from Steve or Maurice and that nothing had changed from what I saw.

That was all that we talked about regarding my stay or return. He knows it's a trial and that I have some reservations. My knee-jerk was to say to him at some point that I would be glad to work with him but not for him. However, I'm less inclined to push that at this time. After spending three days with him, I am impressed with what he brings to the table regarding manufacturing operations. I could work with him, maybe even for him. As it stands, he is head of Synthron Q, with Ilya as head of Synchron Rus. All of the factory operations issues fall under Q. I need to play this one close to the chest and not burn any bridges.

We just did a walk-through of the tool-making facility. It is very impressive, a great place to take the Lucas people. Jim drooled as he saw the examples of form tools they produce. It is typical of Russian manufacturers. They make each plant self-sufficient; in this case, they can do it all, many things required for the operation. Jim feels he can get some real leverage with the stuff needed at Naviins and will bring back a drawing and example of the chuck.

Met with Shmyslaev at 11am (Jim, Khabi, Novikiv, me). Jim started saying that in the states when we play sports or cards with clients, we never win. That comment relates to Bosloviak playing cards with the GD last night, winning about 7000 rubles ($1.40). Jim continued, "very pleased with the program at AA; the people are doing the things they need to do. He would feel better if they had the raw material. Last Saturday, he had a meeting with Cherepovitz on how long it would take to get the raw material. They don't know if they can make it to spec the first time. They propose to make one batch, then adjust as required, which will take a very long time. Jim says if the material is not exactly to spec, he will try to get a deviation from Lucas.

Cherepovets said they had Kulikov, Chistikov, and Maizen visit but have not signed a protocol yet. So he thinks Kogan and Adler will visit in two weeks to address this. One batch equals 60 tons from Servicall (Cherepovitz supplier) at 6.5 million rubles per ton, which is very high. Jim told them he could get it for 700 marks per ton from the Czech Republic, half the Cherpovitz price. They agreed to work the price down as they gained experience. Jim laid out a schedule; if we pay in advance to Cherepovitz by June 5th, it takes five days to make and six days to ship, which means it could ship by July 6th. He further told Shmyslaev they wouldn't sell to AA direct until their debt was paid, but there was a way to work that out with a deal through Synchron. So, it's a $78,000 risk!

Jim then spoke about material from Autobrizdy. He was told they only have material for 10 tons, not for the rest, although that doesn't make sense since the pistons we will make take the place of the pistons now being made at Autobrizdy.

He mentioned the tooling catalog he was given and how impressed he was with the tooling shop. He will pass this on to Lucas to see if we can get tool orders. He then talked about faxing copies to Shymslaev that didn't get to him for days after the fact, pointing out what a big problem this is. He said the new schedule has had four steps added; turning, facing, packaging and shipping. It all assumes the tooling and raw material availability. Every day the raw material is late, the whole schedule will slip the same. So, cropping and the Schuler press must be ready before the material gets here to avoid unnecessary delays.

Jim mentioned his discussion with Krause on the re-submittal of the ISIR documentation. Carl started picking at it when they got on the phone, but Jim said, "stop, Carl, take a deep breath. Just answer one question, are you satisfied with it?" Carl Krause said, "yes!"

The next issue from Smyslaev was regarding the commercial agreement with Synchron. He said they needed a contract copy to get the raw materials imported from the Czech. I called and left a message on Steve's answering machine in Florida saying the same thing earlier today. Many AA people are nervous about not having the Commercial contract signed with Synchron. There is some comfort among Synchron people, having talked with Autobrizdy and faxed a letter from Shmyslaev. They are told the material coming in will be assembled and then shipped back to the origin of the material. I felt like the message to Steve was important since I was very uneasy about it. We will all be gone when the material should arrive this weekend, and I don't want to come back to any problems.

Shmyslaev said maybe we should smuggle the bars in somehow. He then said they could not pay the 318 million rubles for the roller bar material. All the money they have been able to raise now must go to the salaries of his people. There are three possibilities:

1) May get credit from another bank.
2) I Got some possibilities from the Czech Republic people who were here yesterday. However, they are just distributors with customers, which means any cash flow is down the road.
3) Azelka in Moscow is beginning to work again, so we may get some money from them for supplies. However, Khabi says that is just an election ploy (the election is next month with big questions hanging in the wind about Communism or democracy).

We are in big trouble if none of these three things come forward. Shmyslaev says he guesses we need to wait for the election results. No immediate solution.

Jim said there were two other things, 1) he could feel a positive attitude in the plant today. SM says that is the main problem in the plant today. He then said the business plan had been forwarded to the ministry in government. He is not certain it will be easy to get it to the Finance Minister. If it does get there and gets approved, the government will invest 40%. He said that if Moskvich (Azelka) had worked for the last year, they would have had no problem. He talked about making excavators (Caterpillar types), but the buyers have no money. The gas industry and oil industry all have no money.

Jim said that he had made observations in St. Petersburg that there were certainly a lot of people in the stores spending money, but no one seemed to have it. SM said that is true only in Moscow or St. Pete, not in Kineshma or elsewhere.

Khabi talked about moving machining and grinding into the cell for production. Jim said yes, that is a good long-range plan, but not until we get into full production and not to spend money before we have it.

Jim talked about sending Lucas the Corrective Action plan and saying it was 85% done. He told SM that the Khabi had written a procedure for document signing and Synchron presence. Jim, myself, or

Khabi can sign the required documents. Jim does not want any delays due to the absence of a signature. Nothing should wait just because Jim is not here.

Jim closed by saying how badly we need a fax machine. He said, "I don't know the best way to do that." Shmslaev said, "Buy one!" AA will see if they have one. Jim said he was very impressed with the Lucas Gantt chart on the wall in the factory in the cell.

On our way back to the office, we stopped at the office of deputy GD Dogodkin. He is an interesting guy, the consummate Russian. He is a big guy with the kind of sly smile you would expect to see in a Sean Connery spy film. When I first met him a couple of years ago, it was at dinner after our first visit to Avto Agregat. When Ilya went through the normal routine in Russian as to why I wouldn't be sharing in their vodka toasts, Dogodkin said, "Salt Lake City!" with a big sly smile. I haven't heard him use another English word since. I didn't think he spoke any English.

We walked back to the office. Jim met with Zoupnik, who told him he had decided to leave 'Synchron and was actively looking for another job. He had some leads, one at Federal Express. Jim agreed to keep him working at a high-quality level until he found another job. Some he could do at home, e.g., translations, but he must spend at least three days a week in the field.

Oleg Zoupnik is one of the subordinates of Yuri Rubanik, a young man of 27 who is a real quality-oriented guy who speaks good English. He is not against Synchron or anyone in the group; he just wants to be with his wife, who is expecting their first child in September. It had been rumored for a while that he was looking. It was positive for Jim to keep him on. He only asked for very productive workdays for Synchron and at least one week's notice when he will leave. This showed me a side of Jim that is beyond the bluster. He told me privately last week that he was ready to "fire his ass!"

We walked back to the hostel at 1:30. Jim, Leonid and I had lunch at 2, then got into the van for the one-hour train trip to Ermolino. In this small village, the train stops on its way to Ivanovo or St. Petersburg. This is the closest train stop to Kineshma on the route between the two cities. The train makes 16 stops on the way to St. Petersburg. I guess that is why it takes 17 hours in total.

The train got us into St. Petersburg at 11:00 am, about an hour late. The driver picked us up at the station, Leonid took the subway to his home, and Jim and I were let off at Ilya's, where we had a two-hour discussion. Jim gave Ilya the protocol letter and the response to the letter. What it said was Nyet! Ilya said Maurice had just arrived at Koblenz and that Steve didn't know anything about the need for the contract for the material. Regarding Rossochoff, Steve said the draft of the letter to him went to Rossochoff, but Steve didn't fax the letters.

Naviins owes money to Cherepovitz. Adler and Geller went to the material source, who was the top GOST contact. He is a good network contact. He said no one is providing the material today. Still, there are two candidates: 1) Cherepovitz and 2) another in the south of Russia. This is a smaller plant and may be easier to deal with. Jim mentioned on the QT that Severstal would buy Cherepovitz. Rolling mill steel will be best from Cherepovets. Therefore, do both a prime and alternative source.

Ilya said the basic problem with the material is in Steve's head. Four years ago, material in Russia was dirt cheap (1992). Now capacity is the same or less with higher overhead. Now, the material is higher than in the West. We have asked Autobrizdy to see their supplier, told us no. But Ilya wants to strike a deal with the Autobrizdy supplier. I can't get Maurice or Steve to see it. Jim says LTV (a long-time Booz client headquartered in Cleveland) may buy Cherepovitz. Therefore, Steve surely has network contacts to cover this possibility.

Jim stops the discussion: Where are we? We have several partners who had a dream four years ago. We have cornered the dream and have one customer with two suppliers, with 72 purchase orders at Naviins. 1) How did we get the customer?

We put a full-court press and sold the idea to the leader at Lucas. But we didn't develop the Russian suppliers. We have no commercial agreements. Steve and Ilya could spend 24 hours at Avto Agregat and walk away with an agreement. Our customer is pissed off! Ilya explained in detail the tax problems and implications associated with the agreement. Whew!

I am on the train to Moscow from Kineshma. Tomorrow is the election and, therefore, a holiday. I'm on the train with Khabi and Zaitsev. This is a real hoot. They are reading from an English/Russian book, trying English phrases, and laughing at the top of their lungs. Khabi will laugh and ask Zaitsev to read a sentence, then help him with the pronunciation. This is a great experience because I'm doing the same thing, trying to read a book I bought last weekend in Moscow titled Beginning Russian. But I noticed I have only 32 minutes left on my battery.

I met Jim, Leonid, and Ed yesterday in Kineshma. It was to have been a time of huddles to line out the plan to make AA successful. It turned out to be a chaotic time with not so much accomplished. However, I came away with greater respect for Jim and his actions. They left a couple of hours before us on their way to St. Petersburg.

Khabi wants us to open a small office in Moscow. Shipelevski said we could do it at NATI for $300 per month, with phone privileges, etc. Steve fired Shipelevski on the last trip, so I don't know the background. However, it makes a lot of sense since the entire Q team at AA lives in Moscow; Khabi, Zaitsev, Zoupnik, Novikov, and me. Khabi said that if he and I agree, he thinks Furey will follow suit. We will discuss it at the Operations Council in St. Pete on Monday. I chose to stay in Moscow Thursday and Friday to close on the apartment, not returning to AA. Zoupnik will be there on both days, and I have left him a list of tasks to accomplish. Then we will all be back to AA on Tuesday. I need to plan for some recommendations on keeping the noise level down in the AA office and getting more done.

We just had our supper on the train. Zaitsev reached into his satchel and brought out several small plastic bags of goodies, and the three of us went after them like farmhands. It consisted of a fried chicken leg/thigh for each of us, a tomato we ate like an apple, and a cucumber we ate like a carrot, with lots of black Russian bread. He had placed a brown paper across the small table between the train seats that face each other in our compartment designed for four people. Two bunks above the seats we were on, which later served as cots for the night's sleep. They each had half a glass of vodka, while I had fruit juice to go with the meal.

Later the gal who ran the car stopped to see if we wanted coffee or tea. After the greasy meal, all the scraps went into the middle of the table. The paper was folded up and placed into the trash at the end of the car. Also, we had a type of cake popular in kiosks as dessert, waxy chocolate covering with the cake in a foil package so that its shelf life is months at least. Not so good, but still welcome.

Khabi is a very animated speaker with much frustration over his lack of English skills. He emotes handily while eating, poking the chicken leg into the air to make a point, then scowling as he searches for an English word to convince me. This is really a tight little bunch of merry men. Zaitsev is a quiet farmer type. He reminds me of the little rascal with straw in his hair all grown up. He always brings something in his satchel from his garden to eat. On the trip from Moscow Sunday night, he brought a sack of fresh strawberries.

Notes on Kineshma

When we secured the training effort with AA, we had many long weeks in Kineshma. The company had a hostel (small hotel) where we retired after each day's labor at the plant.

My wife and I had a flat in Moscow, a small 5th-floor arrangement, to which I would journey at the end of each week's labor in Kineshma. That put me on the train Thursday nights to Moscow, then Monday nights on the train back to AA.

To Bob's family members

> *Enclosed in this non-original package are some Russian souvenirs to your family from my family and me. Bob was so busy these days, and I hope he had limited time for some souvenirs from Russia. These enclosed things may remind him and the rest of his family of those happy and not-so-happy business days we spent together in my country undergoing the transformation stage.*

EXPAT SECRETS

> *The first thing enclosed is a miniature-size souvenir called SAMOVAR (during the previous time, such vessels the people used to prepare boiled water for tea, the original fuel was wood sticks under the vessel. Later the vessel was transformed, and electric heaters have been used till now. Modern actual SAMOVARS are of big size with a capacity of 3 liters of water provided with electric heaters.*
>
> *The second thing enclosed is an old-fashioned glass cup together with a cup holder which is made of silver. It is preferable after a long storage period to clean the silver cup holder with appropriate silver-cleaning agents or solutions because it may become darker in color.*
>
> *The third thing enclosed is a simple and inexpensive Russian wristwatch (non-automatic); operating instructions are attached. The fourth thing enclosed is a tray together with six miniature cups which not necessarily can be used for alcoholic drinks.*
>
> *And here are some words for the customs personnel in Russian for clearance: (Russian characters)*
> *Best wishes to your family*
> *Pavev Youriev and his family*
> *October 17, 1994."*

This material was left on my doorstep by a member of one of my quality classes in Moscow. Not a small heart-tug from one of many.

Russian Quality Training Awards

During my efforts in Russia, I taught the principles of quality control at two different universities. Students for these efforts were engineers and technologists interested in what Synchron was trying to create in Russia. Following are letters sent to the ASQC, the governing body in the US for all things Quality, commemorating my efforts:

To: American Society for Quality Control 9/18/94
PO Box 3005, Milwaukee, WI 53201-3005

November 2, 1994

Gentlemen:

I have the pleasure to inform you that Mr. Bob Robertson, ASQC Certified Quality Engineer and Vice President of Synchron Consulting, Inc., presented to Russian students ten lectures (each one about four hours) on the topic of: "Quality Audit." This course lasted for about half a year at Moscow Inst. of Automobile Mechanics and Moscow Research Inst. of Tractors and Automobiles. The lectures were given by leading Russian experts working in the area. They were beautiful in form, clear, and very interesting. The course was kept within the ASQC program, and all students received great pleasure from it. At this moment, I am editing the Russian translation of Mr. Robertson's lectures and hope to publish it in Russia.

There is no doubt that these lectures are a very important step to successful cooperation between USA and Russia.

With best wishes, Dr. Yu. Adler
President of the small firm "STAT BFQ."
(STATistics is the Base for Quality")
Editor and publisher of the Russian private journal "The Road to Quality."

EXPAT SECRETS

To ASQC Board 10/17/94

As a President of the Moscow Institute of Electronic Technology (MEIT), I would like to express my appreciation for the wonderful job done by the member of ASQC, Mr. Robert Robertson, in the University in arranging and lecturing at Quality Engineering Classes. Within the framework of these initiatives, Mr. Robertson has delivered a two-semester ASQ CQE course for employees of Zelenograd electronic companies and MIET staff.

We believe that quality issues are of the utmost importance to the Russian economy at the moment. That is why we so much value and praise Mr. Robertson's goodwill and sincere efforts in sharing his vast professional knowledge.

Vitali Verner
President of MIET,
President of the Russian Deming Association

Data Collection

A lengthy manufacturing process involves eight consecutive steps. The output, an electrical parameter, cannot be measured until the final process step is completed – even though the cause of variation within the output may be the raw material used at the first step or in any of the following operations.

The manufacturer found nearly 50% of the output failed to meet customer specifications. So the engineer who designed the process was called in to help find a solution.

The engineer, after consideration, decided that step four might be where the problem originated. When he designed the circuit, he designated a process temperature range from 160 to 180 degrees at this step. However, that designation was somewhat arbitrary and had never been statistically validated.

So he decided to conduct a test. He told the shop foreman to produce three pieces at these temperatures; 160°, 170°, and 180°. "We'll tag each of the nine pieces, so we'll know at which temperature each was produced. Then, when they reach the end of the line, we'll measure the parameter."

The spec for the electrical parameter they would measure at the end of the process was 4.5 units minimum to 6.5 units maximum.

Here's what happened: The first three pieces (#1, #2, and #3) were put through step 4 at 160° at around 9:30 am. The next three (#4, #5, and #6) were put through step 4 at 170° around 10:15 am the same morning. And the last three units (#7, #8, and #9) were put through step 4 at 180° at 11:00 am.

Two days later, when the tagged pieces had become finished products, they were measured. The engineer found that all three pieces produced at 160° were unacceptable. One unit produced at 170° was unacceptable. But at 180°, all three units were acceptable.

$$T1\ (160°) = 2.7, 1.9, 3.6$$
$$T2\ (170°) = 4.2, 3.8, 4.5$$
$$T3\ (180°) = 4.8, 5.7, 5.2$$

So, the engineer raised the temperature at step 4 from 175° to 185°. But the yield remained at only 50%. What went wrong?

ANALYSIS

The *way* the engineer arranged the nine parts when he examined the test results led him to draw a false conclusion. He looked at the measurements for the pieces in the same order they went through step 4: (#1, #2, #3 – – #4, #5, #6 – – #7, #8, #9). But something else was happening in the process while the test was conducted. The engineer's sequence of data was in phase with a non-random pattern. The graph below reveals that pattern. The solid black dots represent the nine pieces tested. The other dots represent reading from units treated within the normal process temperature range.

As we can see, some factor connected to time, not temperature, was the source of variation. The output was more or less steadily rising during the day – – a non-random pattern.

The odds of the numbers 1 through 9 falling into the order 1,2,3,4,5,6,7,8,9 randomly is over 300,000 to 1. However, if we force the sequence into a truly random pattern, we can avoid the engineer's mistake. For example, find a nine-digit random sequence (either from a random numbers table or a calculator or PC), such as the following:

30 93 44 77 33 73 78 80 65

Then assign the part numbers to the random numbers by labeling them according to their ranking from lowest to highest. So now we have:

>(P = Part number)
>30 93 44 77 33 73 78 80 65
>P1 P9 P3 P6 P2 P5 P7 P8 P4
>T1 T2 T3

The same part processed in this sequence would have produced no evident trend:

>T1 (160°) = 2.7, 5.2, 3.6 (avg. = 3.83)
>T2 (170°) = 4.5, 1.9, 3.8 (avg. = 3.40)
>T3 (180°) = 4.8, 5.7, 4.2 (avg. = 4.90)

Randomized sequencing can help separate sources of variation in a multi-step process. If a non-random pattern results, we've found the likely culprit!

CHAPTER 6

Illinois, Nevada, Idaho

6.0 — The Retrofit

At the conclusion of our Russian adventure, I returned to the consulting practice for a couple of years in the states, wrote my first book on the stock market, and attempted to put a web service together selling stock trading materials. However, this was not the end of my Quality Control training work.

According to Brittanica, "Until the 1990s, many computer programs (especially those written in the early days of computers) were designed to abbreviate four-digit years as two digits to save memory space. These computers could recognize '98' as '1998' but would be unable to recognize '00' as '2000.' Many feared that when the clocks struck midnight on January 1, 2000, many computers using an incorrect date would fail to operate properly...."

The concern was that software and hardware failures would lead to widespread chaos following January 1, 2000. "Mainframe computers, including those typically used to run insurance companies and banks, were thought to be subject to the most serious Y2K problems, but even newer systems that used networks of desktop computers were considered vulnerable."

As a closure to my Russian activities, with Avtoagregat's success in Kineshma, I read with interest the current literature, filled with Y2K stories. Long story short, my next job was with State Farm Insurance in Bloomington, IL, bringing my wife and me back to the states for a short assignment.

Britannica continues, "An estimated $300 billion was spent (almost half in the United States) to upgrade computers and application programs to be Y2K-compliant. As the first day of January 2000 dawned and it became apparent that computerized systems were intact, reports of relief filled the news media. These were followed by accusations that the likely incidence of failure had been greatly exaggerated. Those who had worked in Y2K-compliance efforts insisted that the threat had been real. They maintained that the continued viability of computerized systems proved that the collective effort had succeeded. Ultimately, analysts agreed that programming upgrades from the Y2K-compliance campaign had indeed improved computer systems, and that the benefits of these improvements would continue to be seen for some time." (See https://www.britannica.com/technology/Y2K-bug)

After the conclusion of my consulting gigs with the FBI in West Virginia and State Farm in Illinois, and as the Y2K crisis subsided, I answered an ad for a teaching position in Elko, NV, at Great Basic College (GBC), looking ahead to some relative peace. This job was as an Instrumentation Professor, a position that fit my resume nicely as it was a similar position to what I had left at the community college in Milwaukee years before. We spent five years at GBC, working where the gold extraction industry flourished in Northern Nevada. For the last two years there, I worked summers as Instrumentation Instructor at Micron Technology, about five hours north in Boise, ID, where the company put us in housing close to the manufacturing plant during summers.

After the second summer, I chose to work full-time at Micron with my brand of Quality Control technology. During the next ten years, I trained thousands of Micron technologists across the country and at several foreign locations, including Singapore, Catania, and Milan, Italy.

One interesting experience in Singapore where I attended church, a gentleman in the group recognized me from many years ago. He remembered the youth group my wife worked with, where she had outings at our apartment. He remembered the dozens of shoes outside our apartment when my wife had an activity. (In Singapore, you didn't take your shoes inside; they were left outside the door.)

We met in a small bungalow for church back then. Now the church had grown into a three-story building housing four congregations.

Fun-Ditty #6.0

> *"Winners take responsibility, and losers blame others."*
>
> *– Brit Hume*

6.1 – Personalities

Even back in the states, my wife and I continued to face new challenges and expand our knowledge and understanding of true principles that can help us weather life's storms. In a sense, we all need a "retrofit" once in a while. It's not always part of our original makeup to understand the bigger picture, so it's important to keep learning and keep growing. As much as our many adventures were thrilling, they were also stressful and not always easy on our relationship. But occasionally, at just the right times, we would providentially be exposed to insight that helped us make it through another day. On one occasion, that insight came to us through a gifted book that helped us understand our personalities better: *Personality Plus* by Florence Littauer.

Following is a derivative of the book written by Claire Markwood. Its message had a profound effect on us during this chapter of our lives. I count the principles the original book (and this summary) as treasured secrets that can help us all enjoy greater success in industry, business, and life:

> Personalities differ. Knowing this helps us understand ourselves and others better. Considering this can be a valuable insight into managing our lives. We each have the feeling that we expect everyone to feel as we do, to see things as we see them, and to think as we do. How deeply and dogmatically this is felt depends on a person's understanding of why this is and how emotionally mature they are. This seems to be the common denominator in

all levels of conflict. It also has something to do with internal conflict.

Difficulties in relationships are more easily worked through if we understand ourselves first. This leads to a better understanding of others (their basic personality type) and greater success in each relationship. This is most important in the more closely integrated relationships, like with spouses, children, and all the outlaws within our in-law families.

Hippocrates (the Father of Western Medicine) observed the mind-body complex of individuals and classified four major constitutional types, personalities, or mental attitudes, if you will. Much has been written on personalities. Some have divided the types into colors of Blue, Red, White, and Yellow instead of Greek humor. There are other venues as well. All are fun, and all are revealing. My favorite is the Greek thesis, as illustrated in this little parable:

The rabbit was planning a party. Each detail had been perfectly thought out. Lists were made and checked for weeks in preparation. The day had arrived, and although exhausted, Rabbit placed the evenly cut carrot sticks in neat little stacks on each plate. Decorations were done; games were planned and lined up in order of use. His attention to detail, and his need for order and perfection, were often criticized. His expectation was perfection. He was a Melancholic. Rabbit's greatest need was to be understood.

He was hurt and offended when his first guest barged in the door, criticized the seating, and demanded that it be changed now! This was Bear. He had a very organized mind, could look at any situation, rise to any occasion, take charge of any event, and see how it could be done better. He was a natural leader; that is what he did, whether or not anyone wanted him to. Sometimes his decisions were impulsive, but he could bully them into success. Bear was a Choleric. His greatest need was to be followed.

The turtle had ambled in unnoticed. Everyone loved Turtle, and he was always invited. He had a hard shell and never ruffled anyone's feathers. Being invited was a good thing, for his very presence usually kept the peace, and his greatest need was to be included and respected. He was happy and managed his life without noticing much about what anyone else was doing. The turtle was a Phlegmatic. Today, the fray between Rabbit and Bear went unnoticed as he sat in the recliner and poked his head out just enough to see the book he'd brought with him.

Late, as usual, a very pleasant, smiling, chattering and having fun calico kitten bounced in the door. She had run into a group of raccoons and quickly made friends with them. Being in the middle of telling them a very funny story, she brought them along to the party. The rabbit was troubled, as he hadn't planned for them. Bear was getting loud, as they wouldn't sit where he wanted them to. Turtle didn't notice. But Kitten being a Sanguine, WAS noticed. That was her greatest need, and she knew how to make that happen.

There was some civility in this group of raccoons. They were not raucous, but they were bodacious. They upset Rabbit, annoyed Bear, pestered Turtle, and lost interest in Kitten.

Needless to say, this party was a disaster. No one cared but Rabbit. But then it was his party. He wanted to cry, and he did.

Of course, we are all a combination of the Greek personality ethers. Still, we could be predominately more one than the others:

- A Melancholic will worry but will be organized, a perfectionist, which is a flaw.
- A Choleric will act decisively and maybe too rashly, often bossy.

- A Phlegmatic will be a little disorganized and may be forgetful but always pleasant.
- A Sanguine will be distracted and impetuous, always entertaining.

Balanced people have an even combination of the four personality types. They use each part of their personality or developed gifts to make the best of any situation.

This new awareness had a profound impact on our relationship. My wife recognized herself as a Melancholic / Choleric, while I was more inclined to be a Sanguine / Phlegmatic. Not wrong, just different. "Well," we thought, "that explains a lot!"

This new perspective certainly made a difference in my family, but it also helped my work teams get along better as well. Personalities indeed differ. Keen perception of our personality imprint can be a helpful tool in assessing risk tolerance, impulsiveness, commitment, or in short, how we manage our lives.

Fun-Ditty #6.1

> "The difference between the reason of man and the instinct of the beast is this, that the beast does but know, but the man knows that he knows."
> – *John Donne*

6.2 — Hunt for the Red X — The Shainin System

While teaching and developing curriculum in Elko, Nevada, I became fascinated with the work of Dorian Shainin who had published groundbreaking problem-solving strategies that were widely adopted throughout manufacturing, especially in the automotive industry. He coined the term *The Red X*, representing that unknown factor or variable which would be key to a company's success.

As we know in mathematics, X almost always refers to the "unknown" factor. In industry, you want to discover which one factor, when changed, will improve quality, increase productivity, and elevate profits. An important key to discovering the X is in knowing what questions to ask. If we are only allowed to ask questions that can be answered with yes or no, then it is important to find efficient clue-generation strategies.

Shainin's work had many. To demonstrate the power of one of his strategies, he showed that with an unabridged dictionary, you can find any pre-selected word in only 17 steps by opening the dictionary in the middle, looking at the bottom corner and asking, "Is the secret word before the word NONE?" yes or no? He asserted that if you do it again and again by half each time, you'll have your word in 17 steps. This is called a Binary search. By the eleventh step, you will have the word on one page. For me at the time, this was a new paradigm, to realize that a very specific "unknown" could be identified so methodically. Imagine the implications of this in Quality Control.

Shainin's underlying premise could be summed up in two beliefs:

1. That there are dominant causes of variation.
2. That there is a diagnostic and remedial journey.

He suggested that, in any problem, there is a dominant cause of variation, based on the Pareto principle (that 80% of consequences come from 20% of causes). Dominant causes will be major contributors to the defects and must be remedied before there can be an adequate solution. To Shainin, the dominant cause is the Red X.

He recognized that there may be additional large causes, and those also must be dealt with. If, for example, a team uses his system to reduce the number of leaks in engine blocks, they may discover a number of *categories* of leaks, defined by location in the block. By considering leaks at each location as separate problems, they could rapidly determine a dominant cause and a remedy for each problem. This isn't much different from finding the unknown word in a dictionary: break the problem down by location, and you would be following one of the Shainin strategies.

It is using a process of elimination to identify dominant causes. To achieve this, Shainin taught the importance of using *families* of causes of variation, or groups of varying process inputs that act at the same location or at the same time. You can learn more about his system at https://shainin.com.

Finding a root cause requires an element of faith or belief that there *is* something to be found, or that there are unseen factors at play. It reminds me of a poem that had a great impact on me called Soybeans, by Thomas Alan Orr. It affirms that, in many ways, life itself is a mystery, and our success depends on our ability to imagine possibilities, and recognize providential clues that lead the way to help us reach our potential.

I count the things I learned from Shainin as yet another profound secret, because we can use similar processes of elimination to identify the root cause or causes of just about any challenge we face in life. Do you experience the same kind of frustration in multiple friendships? Do you experience the same kind of physical discomfort with certain categories of food? If you are in sales, do you keep hearing the same kind of responses from customers who choose not to purchase? Approaching your challenges methodically to identify common threads and root causes can make a tremendous difference in your ability to learn the lesson each experience contains, and make course corrections to experience greater success in that area.

Fun-Ditty #6.2

> *"Intelligence appears to be the thing that enables a man to get along without education. Education appears to be the thing that enables a man to get along without the use of his intelligence."*
> *– A.E. Wiggan*

6.3 – Pre-suasion

Later in life, I came across an interesting statement by a man named Robert Cialdini who said: "[B]eing perceived as trustworthy is an effective way to increase one's influence and ... it takes time for that perception to develop."

That statement in itself isn't particularly curious; it's what he asserted next that got my attention. He said, "Over the years, I've attended a lot of programs designed to teach influence skills. ...[T]hey've stressed that being perceived as trustworthy is an effective way to increase one's influence and that it takes time for that perception to develop. Although the first of these points remains confirmed, a growing body of influence indicates that there is a noteworthy exception to the second."

I wondered, what is this exception? How can we increase our trustworthiness more quickly? He continued, "It turns out to be possible to acquire instant trustworthiness by employing a clever strategy. Rather than succumbing to the tendency to describe all of the most favorable features of an offer or idea upfront and reserving mention of any drawbacks until the end of the presentation (or never), a communicator who references a weakness early on is immediately seen as more honest."

The author calls this acting "pre-suasively". It's being proactive, authentic, real. People prefer that. He adds, "The advantage of this sequence is that, with perceived truthfulness already in place, when the major strengths of the case are advanced, the audience is more likely to believe them." (Cialdini, Robert. *Pre-Suasion: Persuasive arguments to make some ideas look more positive.* Simon & Schuster, New York, 2016.)

I can affirm that, although I didn't find his work until after I retired, this principle is true and assisted me in profound ways throughout my career as I needed to gain influence with different management sorts, especially in my foreign assignments.

This principle no doubt could help any person enjoy more success in their work, their families, and their community. Be honest. Be forthright. Don't be afraid to reveal weaknesses early, and you may discover that your credibility and influence afterward is much greater than it otherwise would have been.

Fun-Ditty #6.3

> *"The best edge we all have is the freedom to find and develop our own skills. It gives us the freedom to take risks, to try, to fail, to learn, and try again. Mistakes are the mother of all learning, and our daily experience reminds us of that. The joys, the aha's, and tears that follow allow our continued growth."*

6.4 — Constructive Confrontation

Allow me to paint a picture:

The meeting begins. The President outlines a proposed change in which many are opposed to the plan. After a vehement meeting, with all opposing viewpoints aired, what looked like a failure, the adoption of the new proposal, was finally agreed upon. This outcome is even better than the original idea, demonstrating the power of Constructive Confrontation.

In my career, I learned that management can facilitate changes that inevitably alter outdated practices and procedures, changes that inevitably step on some toes. The conflict lies at the heart of managing any business activity. Therefore, confrontation, facing issues over which there is disagreement, cannot be avoided.

Constructive Confrontation (CC) is a problem-solving technique focusing on attacking problems straight out, as opposed to being overly careful, diplomatic, or devious. Its two most important features are directness and immediacy.

If we don't face an ongoing problem, stress builds. Statements such as "It won't work because...." can make the necessary meaningful dialogue possible. CC has nothing to do with being polite or rude – it is instead a direct and immediate way of dealing with problems.

It needs to be handled in a business-like manner, even while the substance taken up is a matter of intense mutual concern. While CC can be learned, it can be difficult to practice. Many find that it produces pain initially, because most have been brought up to be polite. However, CC must be incorporated to initiate specific and positive problem-solving actions.

We must concentrate on the problem, not the people involved. If a piece of machinery breaks down and ruins everything, was it because the equipment was not maintained properly, or was it because its operator was not properly trained? Or was it something else altogether? We must dig out the truth before we can take intelligent corrective action.

If CC becomes personal, the reaction will be personal, and focus on the problem will be lost. Bringing problems into the light as soon as possible enhances not just corporate health, but the health of relationships in our personal and social lives as well.

Fun-Ditty #6.4

> "I have three precious things which I hold fast and prize. The first is gentleness; the second is frugality; the third is humility, which keeps me from putting myself before others. Be gentle and you can be bold; be frugal and you can be liberal; avoid putting yourself before others and you can become a leader among them."
>
> – Lao-Tzu

CONCLUSION

So, how does this story end? After a long career with twists and turns I never expected, it ends with us back in the states with four magnificent children, 22 magnificent grandchildren, and six greats (but they are all great), spread from New England to the Southwest. Our adventures as an expat family stretched us and taught us many things. It is good now to rest and reflect on the wonders of life, of true principles on which we can depend, and of all the good Lord has done for us. Through it all we learned the truth of this final Fun-Ditty, with which I will close:

Fun-Ditty #7

> *"Not armies, not nations, have advanced the race, but here and there, in the course of the ages, an individual has stood up and cast his shadow over the world."*
>
> *- Edwin H. Chapin.*

What more can I say? What I can say, what I must say, is a heartfelt tribute to the companion who has stood ready to move camp with family and household more times than I can count. We've been together over 60 years, and counting. My dear wife, I love you!

The End

BONUS FUN-DITTIES

"Work is love made visible. And if you cannot work with love but only with distaste, it is better that you should leave your work and sit at the gate of the temple and take alms of those who work with joy."
- Kahlil Gibran

"God gives every bird its food, but he does not throw it into the nest."
- Josiah Gilbert Holland

"An ounce of mother is worth a pound of clergy."
- Spanish proverb

"Reading after a certain time diverts the mind too much from its creative pursuits. Any man who reads too much and uses his own brain too little falls into lazy habits of thinking."
- Albert Einstein

"How old would you be if you didn't know how old you were?"

— Satchell Paige

"Noise proves nothing. Often a hen who has merely laid an egg cackles as if she had laid an asteroid."

— Mark Twain

"Education makes a people easy to lead, but difficult to drive; easy to govern, but impossible to enslave."

— Henry Brougham

"Education today, more than ever before, must see clearly the dual objectives: education for living and education for making a living."

— James Mason Wood

"The only people who achieve much are those who want knowledge so badly that they seek it while the conditions are still unfavorable. Favorable conditions never come."

— Clive S. Lewis

"Don't gamble; take all your savings and buy some good stock and hold it till it goes up, then sell it. If it don't go up, don't buy it."
— Will Rogers

"There will never be a really free and enlightened state until the state comes to recognize the individual as a higher and independent power, from which all its own power and authority are derived, and treats him accordingly."
— Henry David Thoreau

"The trouble with the American public is that it thinks something is better than nothing."
— Alfred Stieglitz

"Life would have been infinitely happier if we could only be born at the age of eighty and gradually approach eighteen."
— Mark Twain

ABOUT THE AUTHOR

Bob Robertson is a retired professional quality engineer and educator with extensive experience in manufacturing environments throughout the world, including Singapore, Indonesia, Russia, Italy, and various locations throughout the United States.

Over the course of his career he was an electrical engineer, statistical consultant, tenured professor of instrumentation, published author, professional educator, university course developer, and equities trader. At the time of this printing, Bob and his wife were the parents of four, grandparents of twenty-two, and great-grandparents of six.

www.ingramcontent.com/pod-product-compliance
Lightning Source LLC
Chambersburg PA
CBHW071359160426
42811CB00115B/2431/J